THE
EXPECTED GOALS
PHILOSOPHY

THE EXPECTED GOALS PHILOSOPHY

A Game-Changing Way
of Analysing Football

JAMES TIPPETT

First published in 2019

Published in the United Kingdom

The Expected Goals Philosophy

©James Tippett

Printed in Great Britain

ISBN: 978-1-08988-318-0

CONTENTS

PREFACE

When I tell people that I used to log stats for a betting consultancy, they usually assume that my role was to record the number of passes, tackles, corners and such actions that take place in a football match. These are the typical statistics that people think of when they hear the term "football data". In fact, I was tasked with recording none such metrics. My job was simply to measure the danger level of each attack which took place. Essentially, the only information I had to collect was Expected Goals data.

I first came across the Expected Goals method whilst working at Smartodds, a company who collect data on football matches and sell the statistics to high-rolling professional gamblers. These clients use the information to inform their betting. Essentially, Smartodds base their success on their ability to analyse football more accurately than the bookmakers. Through more accurately gauging the performance levels of teams, Smartodds have been able to turn over hundreds of millions of pounds through betting on the outcome of matches.

The company don't own more powerful computers than the bookmakers. They don't possess insider knowledge, or a more intelligent cohort of analysts than the bookies. Smartodds' edge comes from the metric which they use to analyse football: The Expected Goals method.

In a sport as random, as unpredictable and as luck-inducing as football, the Expected Goals method (otherwise referred to as "xG") is by far and away the most useful tool for discerning what *actually* happened on the field of play. Whilst working at Smartodds, I was given an insight into the Expected Goals method and its potentially revolutionary impact on the game. My stint at the company began in 2015, when xG was only prevalent in the deep, dark corners of football analytics. People didn't know about xG back then. I became fascinated by this revolutionary, yet completely unknown, way of analysing the sport.

When I left the company in 2016 to go to university, I began collecting my own Expected Goals data. I would watch Premier League matches and use my training from Smartodds to assess the probability of each attack resulting in a goal. This data allowed me to achieve success in my own personal gambling.

I managed to get into the university football team, and often found myself explaining the Expected Goals method to my teammates. By this point, the media had begun slowly incorporating xG stats into their broadcasts and across their various social media outlets. A lot of people had started to hear about xG, but still didn't really understand it. I would try to explain it to them. I'd tell them that it had been used by professional gamblers to turn over hundreds of millions of pounds. I would tell them that it had been used by clubs to identify hidden gems in the transfer market. I would tell them that analysts had used it to provide a more accurate gauge of team and player performance. They would want to know more, but didn't know where to start. And I wouldn't really know in which direction to point them.

That's why I have written this book. Hopefully it will show the history of how the Expected Goals method rose to prominence. Hopefully it will explain how the Expected Goals method can be used to analyse football. And hopefully it might forecast what the future has in store for Expected Goals.

The Football Code, my previous book, studies basic statistical phenomena that we regularly overlook when analysing football, how our biases affect our prediction-making, why pundits are actually the worst footballing forecasters and how we can turn the tables on the bookmakers. It also briefly explores the Expected Goals method. However, there are several reasons why I now find myself writing *The Expected Goals Philosophy.*

Firstly, I feel that the metric which lends itself to the title of this work is so important, so significant and so potentially revolutionary to the sport of football that a single, focused piece of work must be written to completely encapsulate the philosophy. There are so many aspects to the Expected Goals method, so many ways it can be utilised. Whilst *The Football Code* looked at how we can generally make better footballing predictions, *The Expected Goals Philosophy* seeks to offer a full education on the most ground-breaking means of analysis football has seen.

Secondly, it is incredibly hard to promote change within the beautiful game. Those lobbying for analytics to become more mainstream have been met with stiff opposition. It seems that the average football fan is too disinterested, lazy or, dare I say, ignorant, to accept a more analytical philosophy. Their eyes glaze over as soon as the word 'metric' is uttered. A codified piece of work is needed to bring Expected Goals to the attention of the everyday supporter.

Thirdly, the analytical landscape has changed considerably since I wrote *The Football Code*. In late 2017, huge steps were taken by the footballing world. Media companies finally awoke from their slumber and started paying attention to Expected Goals data. *Match of the Day* started to display xG stats on their broadcasts, whilst Sky Sports also began sharing Opta's Expected Goals information across various platforms. Despite the media's fairly poor explanations of what xG is and how it can be used, this was certainly a ground-breaking advancement for statistical analysis within football. There finally seems enough interest in the Expected Goals method to warrant a book fully devoted to it.

INTRODUCTION

This book will ask the reader to put themselves into the shoes of a professional gambler. You are sitting at your trading desk, trying to make sense of one of the most complicated sports in existence. You are faced with a series of problems. Which teams are better than the other teams? How can you tell which teams are actually good and which are simply lucky? What metrics can you use to better predict future results? Who should you put your money on to win in the next round of fixtures?

This book will also ask the reader to put themselves into the shoes of the Chief Scout at a professional football club. You are sitting in your office, faced with a series of similar problems. How can you tell which players are performing better than others? Which data points separate the skilled players from the lucky ones? In a sport as complex and dynamic as football, how do you even begin to analyse what is happening out on the field of play? Who are the undervalued talents whom your team might be able to sign for rock bottom prices?

In both these roles you are tasked with separating truth from falseness. Separating right from wrong. Separating skill from luck. When it comes to football, these are very difficult things to do. You are surrounded by so much noise, so many opinions, so much misleading data. Hopefully this book will teach you how one simple tool, the Expected Goals method, can answer these questions.

This book is for the "thinking fan". It is intended for those who are tired of old clichés. It seeks to address some of the glaring inefficiencies we harbour when we attempt to analyse and predict football. This book should be approached with an open mind. Any presupposed prejudices should be set aside at this point. If this is done, the contents have the potential to change your outlook on football.

The Expected Goals method is not simply a statistic which can be used to analyse performance. It is a philosophy that challenges the rigid, entrenched and outdated way we talk about the beautiful game. There is, of course, a science to the way we analyse football. But there is also an art. Hopefully this book will reconcile the beauty of football with methodical enquiry.

This book aims to share a new, smarter language with which fans, pundits and players can talk about football. Like all languages, it takes a while to learn and to integrate into our native vocabulary. However, it is necessary that we do so. The dialect which we currently use to talk about the sport is deeply flawed. It is inaccurate at describing what we really mean, and is inefficient when it comes to predicting future events.

Whilst sports such as baseball, basketball, cricket and hockey have embraced the introduction of a more mathematical approach, football has been sceptical of such methods. There are a number of reasons why analytics has struggled to permeate the world's most popular sport. First and foremost, football is incredibly steeped in tradition. The sport has survived over a century without the Expected Goals method, so why do we need it now? Radical ideas are naturally met with such skepticism.

Second, those who have influence within the world of football tend to be less educated than the average person. There is good reason for this. In order to become a professional footballer, an occupation that an overwhelmingly large number of people aspire to attain, one must dedicate all of their time to playing the sport from a very young age. The vast majority of players leave school at sixteen in order to pursue their dream. If they spend time in the classroom learning Pythagoras and Shakespeare whilst others are out on the training pitches, they will be left behind. Thus, footballers tend to be less educated, and therefore less likely to understand (or be willing to understand) more scientific approaches to the beautiful game.

Additionally, those vocations that have influence within the footballing sphere (managers, coaches, pundits, etc.) tend to be comprised of former players. Less intelligent ex-professionals dominate the inner realms of the sport, whilst the smarter analysts find themselves struggling to have their voices heard. A newspaper would rather have a notable former player write their columns than some unheard of mathematician talking about Expected Goals. A television broadcaster would rather cover a ranting manager than hear the opinion of a studious analyst assessing a team's xG output. When it comes to football, and football media in particular, it is more important to be recognisable than to be intelligent.

The noticeable absence of a smart, analytical and scientific voice in the mainstream football media reflects onto the fans who follow such broadcasting. Stupidity breeds stupidity. Thus, supporters are denied exposure to a more intelligent means of analysing the sport. That being said, the Expected Goals method is hardly advanced mathematics. In order to understand the philosophy laid out in this book, the reader simply requires an open mind and the mathematic understanding of a fourteen-year-old.

This book is intended for those who want to attain a deeper understanding of football. The Expected Goals method allows us to more accurately separate the skill and luck of players, managers and teams. It gives us a greater insight into what *should* have happened, rather than what *actually* happened. It asks us to consider the difference between *performances* and *results*. Readers who are disinterested in a more advanced study of the sport, or who are too entrenched in the "traditional" outlook of the beautiful game, will struggle with the contents of *The Expected Goals Philosophy*. This work is aimed at those who are willing to embrace new approaches to the sport, those who are prepared to question everything they know about the beautiful game and those who are interested in the pioneering methods that are changing the way football is being played.

The overarching intention of this book is to explain the Expected Goals method, whilst simultaneously showing how it can be applied. It will study the battle between the traditionalists and the innovators. It will explore why football is such an unfair sport, why better teams often lose and worse teams often win. It will seek to find out how success can turn works of luck into works of genius. Most importantly, it will outline how the Expected Goals method can help us answer some of the sport's most prevalent questions. Who is the best player in the world? What is the key to scouting and signing hidden gems? How can poor teams compete with clubs of far greater wealth? I hope the reader takes as much joy in reading *The Expected Goals Philosophy* as I did in writing it.

1

EXPECTED GOALS

*What to Expect
When You're Expecting Goals*

What is the Expected Goals Method?

Fans make several subconscious judgements whenever they watch a football match. Most routinely, they form an opinion of which team is playing better. Does the scoreline accurately reflect the performance level of each side? Should one team have scored more goals than they actually have? In other words, has luck had a considerable impact on the outcome of the match?

Football is a sport riddled with randomness. Bad teams will often defeat good teams, bad players will often go through patches of playing well and bad managers will often end up in charge of high profile clubs. The damaging effects of chance make football an incredibly hard sport to understand. The Expected Goals method is a tool which we can use to separate the skilful from the lucky and more accurately gauge performance levels.

Put simply, xG tells us the quantity and quality of chances that each team creates from a match. When we look back on results, we often have strong opinions over which side played better. '*If we had scored that penalty we would have won*'. '*They were so lucky to have scored that deflected shot from long-range*'. '*We created so many good chances, how did we lose?*' We base our view of who should have won on the scoring opportunities that were created during the match. Expected Goals data is simply a way of quantifying these scoring chances.

Football is heavily centred around goals. Match reports generally focus on the opportunities that each team created. Highlight packages centre around the openings that each team carved out. Commentators get most excited when a team is about to score. Football revolves around goals, and goals can only occur when teams create scoring opportunities. Indeed, every tactic ever created represents a coach's attempt to develop his team's ability to create chances, whilst at the same time improving their ability to not concede chances. A football match is essentially a series of attacks from each team on the other team. The sides who have the highest quantity *and highest quality* of attacks are clearly the best sides. This is what the Expected Goals method measures.

However, goals are almost as rare as they are important. Thousands of actions take place over the course of each match – in fact, Opta's data collectors suggest that an average of 3,000-4,000 events such as passes, tackles, duels, saves and so on happen over a ninety-minute period. Only a handful of these actions will be shots that result in goals (the average number of goals per match is around 2.7). Each one of the thousands of in-play events is geared towards one thing: chance creation. Assessing the nature of the chances that each team created will reveal which side has deserved to win, regardless of the *actual* scoreline.

The Expected Goals method cuts right through to the core of football thinking. The ability of sides to threaten the opposition goal, whilst simultaneously preventing danger to their own goal, is what separates good teams from bad teams.

HOW IS EXPECTED GOALS CALCULATED?

Essentially, xG indicates how many goals a team could have expected to score based on the quantity and quality of chances that they created in a match. Fans often come away from football matches thinking, "We created much better chances then the opposition, we definitely should have won". The Expected Goals metric is a way of quantifying these scoring opportunities, allowing a better insight into the ability of teams than the *actual* scoreline does.

Teams are often judged by the *quantity* of shots that they have in a match, or indeed in a season. Media companies will show the stats for how many attempts at goal each side has taken in a game. The central premise of xG is that the *quality* of those shots is of equal importance as the quantity. Analysts can work out the number of goals that a team would have expected to score from a certain amount of shots of a certain quality. Similarly, analysts can work out which players have scored more chances than they would be expected to.

Expected Goals data is collected by several different data companies, football clubs and betting firms. The main provider of xG stats to media companies is Opta Sports, who claim to collect the most complete dataset for the Premier League, English Football League, Scottish Professional Football League and many other divisions across the globe. Opta's data experts have analysed over 300,000 shots to calculate the likelihood of an attempt being scored from a specific position on the pitch during a particular phase of play.

Expected Goals works by measuring the likelihood of each shot resulting in a goal. Each effort at goal which takes place in a match has a "Shot Probability" value. For instance, a shot from 30 yards out through a crowd of players may only have a 2% chance of hitting the back of the net, giving it a value of 0.02(xG). On the other hand, a shot into an open goal from six yards out might have a 95% chance of being scored, resulting in a value of 0.95(xG).

At the end of any given match, the Shot Probabilities from either side are added up to reveal the Expected Goals scoreline from a match. For example, suppose that Arsenal play against Manchester City. The London side have six shots over the course of the match, but they are all long shots from distance with a Shot Probability value of 0.1(xG). The Gunners will have amassed a total Expected Goals score of 0.6(xG). Over the course of the same match, Man City only have two shots at goal, but they are both from close range. Suppose that one shot is worth 0.3(xG) and the other is worth 0.4(xG). Man City's Expected Goals score over the course of the ninety minutes is 0.7(xG). Thus, the xG scoreline from the match would be *Arsenal 0.6(xG) – 0.7(xG) Man City*[1]. The scoreline would reflect the fact that Manchester City performed narrowly better than their London counterparts.

There is a natural question which follows: how do you determine the probability of a shot's success? The *location* of a shot has a large bearing on how likely it is to result in a goal. A shot which is taken from a wide position, thirty yards out from goal, will only have a small chance of going in. On the other hand, a close-range shot from a central position will have a high probability of scoring.

An analyst could look at a large sample of past shots taken from an exact position and find how many beat the goalkeeper. Say an analyst looked at 1,000 shots taken from the exact position at the right-hand corner of the penalty area (we are assuming the analyst has a large database of shots spanning across several divisions

---

1   As we will see, this xG scoreline actually occurred between the two teams in November 2017. Manchester City actually won the game by three goals to one, prompting Arsène Wenger to come under fire in his post-match press conference. The Frenchman referenced the Expected Goals scoreline (**Arsenal 0.6(xG) – 0.7(xG) Man City**) in an attempt to outline how close the game had actually been. The two teams had been evenly matched, but the visitors had had luck on their side.

and several seasons. Thousands of shots are taken each season, each one being recorded by companies like Opta. These companies can draw upon vast databases of past shots in order to determine Expected Goals probabilities). Suppose only 50 of these shots ended up in a goal. He could conclude that future shots from this location have a 5% chance of beating the goalkeeper (as 50/1000 previous shots from this position hit the back of the net). Thus, the Expected Goals value from this position is 0.05(xG).

Whilst the location of a shot forms the main basis of its danger level, other factors also play their part. Shots which come from crosses are considerably harder to convert than shots which take place when the ball is standing still. Whether the shot is headed, volleyed or hit from the ground also affects its chance of success. So too does it matter whether the effort is taken on a player's weaker foot. Analysts account for a whole range of such factors in their Expected Goals models.

The above description is a very brief introduction into how to collect Expected Goals data, but hopefully the reader can already get a sense of how it can be used to analyse football. Teams who are consistently creating high value chances are clearly dangerous opposition, whilst those who are only clocking low xG Shot Probabilities evidently lack potency going forward. Similarly, an analyst can work out how many goals a player would have expected to score based on the quality of chances that he has received. If a striker is scoring lots of goals from difficult positions, we might applaud him. Conversely, if a player is drastically underperforming his Expected Goals output, we might question his ability.

WHY IS THE EXPECTED GOALS METHOD IMPORTANT?

Every judgement, opinion or prediction that we make about the beautiful game is grounded on our assessments of past performances. But how can we expect to accurately analyse the sport when it is so considerably determined by luck? This is where the Expected Goals method steps in, providing an antidote to the disease of randomness which permeates football. It is at the forefront of a smarter, more analytical football philosophy.

In recent years, Expected Goals has been used by various establishments in order to facilitate a better understanding of the sport. The more innovative football clubs have begun using xG in several regards. Most obviously, they use it to measure the performances of their own team and players. Has their side been achieving the results expected of them? Do they actually deserve to be where they are in the league table? How efficient have they been at creating chances and preventing the opposition from creating scoring opportunities?

The scouting teams at clubs also use xG data to uncover and sign hidden gems; players who are undervalued by the rest of the footballing world. Certain English clubs have managed to consistently sign great players for low prices because of their Expected Goals tools. This analytical style of recruitment has allowed teams to enjoy great success on shoe-string budgets. We will study the methods of these teams later in the book.

A different type of institution has also utilised the immense predictive ability of the Expected Goals method. Professional gambling syndicates have used xG to calculate accurate probabilities of events occurring. These companies use Expected Goals data to generate odds, which they compare to the bookmakers' odds. The success of their businesses depends on their ability to make more accurate forecasts than the bookies. The Expected Goals method has allowed them to do this. Later, we will more closely examine the top secret gambling cohorts who have turned over millions of pounds through utilising xG.

Fans have finally begun to pay an increasing amount of attention to Expected Goals stats. Slowly but surely, the media have taken notice of this increase in interest. Football supporters are insatiable consumers of facts. In a sport where knowledge is power, Expected Goals is slowly emerging as the most authoritative form of data. In later sections, we will see how the media have entered the early stages of the xG revolution, what problems they have faced in incorporating it into their broadcasts and where the future may lie for supporter interaction. I am confident that, in a few years' time, it will be impossible to read a match report without finding a reference to the Expected Goals scoreline from the game.

The increased exposure which the metric has seen over the last couple of years is simply a drop in the ocean of what is to come. The reason why is simple: *Every footballing judgement ever made is based on an analysis of the performance of teams or players.* And the Expected Goals method offers by far the most advanced, profound and accurate gauge of performance.

Soon, those who do not understand or pay attention to xG data will be left behind. The Expected Goals method allows you to speak about football in a more intelligent language.

"Isn't X an incredible manager?!"
No, xG shows that his team have incredibly lucky to get the results that they have.

"How could Y's defence play so badly?!"
Actually, the Expected Goals data shows that they played very well.

"Why does Z keep missing absolute sitters?!"
Sorry to correct you, but xG suggests that this player is actually scoring more goals than would be expected of him.

Too often in football, the result dictates the narrative. A team who plays badly and wins has "a great mentality" and is able to "grind out results even when not playing well". However, a team who plays badly and loses will be deemed to have obvious flaws. Both of these teams have performed at the same level (i.e. badly), but notice how our analysis has been changed dependent on their result. In order to avoid being fooled by randomness, we should direct more attention to the Expected Goals totals amassed from each game. This will allow us to assess *performances,* rather than *results.*

Only when we fully embrace the Expected Goals method can pundits begin to more accurately comment of football. Only then can managers give more reasonable post-match interviews. Only then can the fans select the best players for their fantasy teams. Only then can we haul football out of the dark ages and into a more intelligent era of analysis.

2

FOOTBALL
PHILOSOPHERS

Traditionalists Versus Revolutionaries

"The Most Useless Stat in the History of Football"

Jeff Stelling is one of the most popular television pundits worldwide. His charm and charisma make him an affable media personality. However, on one afternoon in November 2017, he went on an uncharacteristic rant that sparked debate throughout the world of football. Manchester City had just defeated Arsenal three-one and Arsène Wenger had cited the Expected Goals data from the match in his post-match press conference. The Gunners manager highlighted that Arsenal had amassed 0.6(xG), whilst Man City had accumulated a marginally higher total of 0.7(xG). This reflected the fact that the Manchester side only performed slightly better than their London counterparts. The xG data suggested that the actual scoreline considerably flattered Man City.

Stelling was belligerent in his disapproval of the statistic. "He's the first person I've ever heard to take notice of Expected Goals, which has to be the most useless stat in the history of football", the pundit exclaimed. "What does it tell you? The match finished 3-1, why do you show Expected Goals afterwards? It's absolute nonsense, it really is." Stelling's reaction was met with audible laughter from the rest of the *Soccer Saturday* panel, with Soccer AM later sharing the video on Twitter. Stelling is an influential figure within football. His mocking of the Expected Goals method sparked widespread criticism of the statistic from fans. The incident outlines the scepticism of mathematical methods that exists within the sport.

The Expected Goals method has struggled to permeate mainstream football knowledge and conversation for three fundamental reasons. Firstly, there is an underlying ignorance. This stems from the lack of exposure which analytical methods gain in the media. Football fans are not given a chance to engage with clever means of assessing the beautiful game, and thus are ignorant to the revolutionary impacts that they could have.

Secondly, many fans are simply not interested in statistical analysis. Unfortunately, not everyone will care about a more intelligent approach to football. Fans generally support their team for the social aspect, to give themselves common ground with an overwhelmingly large community of worldwide supporters. Many fans care more about drinking pints before the match than they do about examining their striker's mathematical level of performance. And that's fine. Not everyone wishes to be intelligible on such matters. Ignorance is bliss. There is nothing wrong with going to football simply to slate the referee and have a fun day out. If you have picked up this book, then you are probably interested in understanding more about the sport.

The final reason why a traditionalist might reject more scientific means of analysis is incompetence. It must be confessed, however, that incompetence is irrefutably linked with the previous two reasons. I strongly believe that *every football fan has the ability to understand the philosophy outlined in this book*. It isn't rocket science. A lot of people, especially football fans, automatically switch off when faced with what could be described as a "mathematical approach". The methods outlined in this book could be understood by a schoolchild. As long as the topics are approached with an open mind, every fan has the capability of grasping the concept of the Expected Goals method.

So, for what reason did Jeff Stelling refuse to engage with xG? He certainly isn't ignorant. The fact that he was talking about the Expected Goals method proves that he has at least heard of it. He certainly shouldn't have been disinterested. It is his job to attempt to understand all footballing matters to the best of his abilities. And he certainly isn't incompetent. He is a very intelligent man and certainly competent enough to understand the workings of xG.

Perhaps there is a fourth reason for football's unwillingness to accept the Expected Goals method. *Fear.*

"THE FIRST THROUGH THE WALL ALWAYS GETS BLOODY"

"There is an epidemic failure within the game to understand what is really happening", says Peter Brend, assistant general manager at the Oakland Athletics baseball team in Aaron Sorkin's film adaptation of Michael Lewis' famous book, *Moneyball*. Oakland's financial disadvantage to other teams in the league meant they had to play by different rules in order to achieve the same success. If they hadn't innovated, adapted and gambled, their final position in the table would have ultimately reflected their financial situation and they would have been rooted to the bottom of the league.

The central hypothesis of *Moneyball* is that the traditional methods used by baseball insiders (in particular those of managers, coaches and scouts) over the past century were subjective and often flawed. Statistics such as stolen bases, runs batted in and batting average, typically used to gauge player ability, were relics of a 19th-century view of the game and the statistics available at that time. Billy Beane, the man in charge of player recruitment for the Oakland A's, believed that the future of baseball lay in a broader statistical approach based on numerical models. He realised that the traditional scouting methods used by every other team were outdated, and played this to the advantage of the Oakland

A's. They developed more analytical gauges of player performance in order to field a team that could better compete against their wealthy opponents.

Beane was tasked with recruiting players for the A's, in the same way a Chief Scout might be tasked with recruiting talent for an English football club. He employed the services of Paul DePodesta, who had just graduated from Harvard with a degree in Economics. Together they developed a system of finding undervalued baseball players, whom they could purchase for little money but who could have a large positive impact on the team's performance. At first, Beane's revolutionary and previously unheard of methods were met with rigid opposition; not only from outsiders but also from the other management staff of the Oakland A's. Beane was on the verge of losing his job, before a miraculous turn-around saw the A's embark on a twenty-match winning run.

Beane endured an initial period of difficulty after implementing his radical, mathematical philosophy at Oakland. The A's struggled, and Beane and his analytical team faced ridicule from all corners of the baseball world. It was argued that '*you cannot measure the size of a player's heart*', and that '*baseball is poetry, not mathematics*'. (Incidentally, both these arguments have also been made in order to undermine the progress of statistical analysis within football). Beane came into particular conflict with the manager of the Oakland A's, Art

Howe. Howe refused to play the players that Beane recommended to him because of a scepticism towards the general manager's mathematical methods. For instance, Beane's calculations showed that playing Scott Hatteburg at first base would increase Oakland's chances of victory. However, Howe went with the seemingly obvious choice of Carlos Pena because it would be "easier to explain in job interviews" come the end of the season – the manager was more focused on his reputation than on the performance of his team.

Beane's revolutionary analytical philosophy took time to gain traction. However, after the initial period of struggle, Oakland's innovative approach turned the sport of baseball on its head. Within a handful of seasons, every team in the NBL had adopted the methods outlined in Michael Lewis' *Moneyball*. Beane's success was founded on a previously overlooked statistic: *on-base percentage (OBP)*. His team discovered, following rigorous statistical analysis, that OBP was a far better indicator of offensive ability than the traditional stats used to measure batting talent. Beane realised that a player's ability to get on base was a quality much cheaper to attain in the open market than more historically valued qualities such as speed and contact. This gave the Oakland A's an edge when scouting players, allowing them to compete on a much stricter budget than their competitors. However, it also contradicted conventional baseball wisdom, disproving the beliefs of Oakland's scouts, Art Howe and the sport's media.

———⎯⎯∞∞∞⎯⎯———

Billy Beane's decision to adopt a mathematical philosophy at Oakland demonstrates how traditionalists and revolutionaries can come into conflict. Just as Jeff Stelling refused to accept the Expected Goals method as a form of analysis in football, Art Howe and his scouts refused to accept on-base percentage data as a form of analysis in baseball. Perhaps the main reason for the rejection of scientific methods within sport is fear, or (more specifically) a fear of being replaced. This was certainly the case amongst Oakland's scouting team. The recruitment department were worried that their skill for spotting talent could just as easily be done by a number-crunching computer, prompting them to try and undermine such an approach.

Stelling's rejection of Expected Goals stems from a different type of fear. The job of a sports pundit, to a certain extent, is to tell the television audience what they want to hear. For Stelling, rejecting the Expected Goals method, a new type of analysis which questions the conventional wisdom of football, is much easier than advocating it. The *Soccer Saturday* host's enraged rant about the metric went viral, being shared thousands of times on social media. A clip of him advocating and explaining the statistic would not have been nearly as popular. In fact, it probably would have sparked widespread ridicule from Sky's audience.

This is where the football media fails its fans. Jeff Stelling has the influence to make people listen, to evoke change within the sport, but instead he chose to tell people what they wanted to hear. The Expected Goals method is certainly the most profound form of football analysis, as proven by the success it has brought professional clubs and gambling syndicates alike. However, influencers within the sport are more concerned with being popular than in being radical. *Football needs influential people to go against the herd from time to time, in order to promote intelligent debate within the sport.* The sport is currently spoken about in clichés. Nothing new or innovative comes to the fore because pundits, the people who carry authority within the sport, speak in safe and tiresome platitudes.

Meanwhile, those people who truly understand the power of Expected Goals (such as bettors and scouts) actively try to keep their methods secret. It is within their interest to not promote the Expected Goals method, thus maintaining their edge over the competition. If you had the recipe to make the world's tastiest cake, you wouldn't publish it for everyone to see. You would use it to bake and sell as many products as you could. The Expected Goals method is football's tastiest means of analysis, but the media are worried that it is too different from the current flavours enjoyed by consumers. Fans are still enjoying the current batch of goodies that the media are serving up to them, blissfully unaware of the tastier treats being enjoyed by bettors and professional football clubs.

3

A History of Football Analytics

How the Beautiful Game Evolved

THE HISTORY OF CHARLES REEP

Before we further study the Expected Goals method, it might be useful to reflect on the journey that has led us to where we are now. We can trace the beginning of the football analytical movement to an unlikely source: a man watching an uninspiring Swindon Town side at the County Ground in 1950. On one particular evening, the thousands of home fans packed inside the stadium were growing increasingly frustrated with their team's inability to break down a rigid Bristol Rovers defence. A spectator named Charles Reep found Swindon's languid forward movement particularly vexing. The RAF Wing Commander was so dissatisfied with what he saw that he decided to note down the second half's attacks and attempt to analyse where the side were going wrong. From that point, Reep made quite the habit out of logging games. In fact, he continued to make notes on matches for over forty years.

Born in Cornwall in 1904, Reep trained as an accountant before becoming a founding father of the analytical movement. He would keep track of games by using a pencil and a notebook, and developed shorthand codes for events such as passes, shots and turnovers. The detail with which Reep collected his data was extraordinary. Each pass in the game was classified and recorded by its length, direction, height and outcome, as well as the positions on the pitch where the pass originated and ended. Over the course of his career, Reep's appetite for analysis led him to annotate more than 2,200 fixtures. Incredibly, each match would take eight hours to fully scrutinise.

Following an intense analysis of his data, Reep concluded that moves consisting of three or less passes were more likely to result in a goal than longer passing plays. To him, it made sense that attacking teams should look to get the ball forward as quickly as possible. Reep argued that wingers should remain as high up the pitch as they could, almost on the touchline, waiting for long balls out of defence. These primitive findings are credited with the invention of, and continued fascination with, the English long-ball game.

Reep's conclusions were eventually proven inaccurate, his interpretation of the data was incorrect. The direct approach that Reep championed is clearly not the all-conquering tactic that he perceived it to be. (In actuality, teams would frequently score from shorter passing plays because they would win the ball high up the pitch, close to the opposition goal – not because long balls were the most effective means of attacking play. This is reflected in the modern game, as teams have developed tactics to press intensely and set traps for the opposition high up the pitch). However, whilst Reep's analysis of the stats may have been flawed, his data collection methods were ahead of his time. His logging of the number and nature of passes paved the way for modern football's analysts.

THE HISTORY OF OPTA

Opta Sports are the world leaders in sports data. The company collect and supply detailed stats which brings sports content and coverage to life. When a Sky Sports commentator quotes a player's passing percentage, the media company will have probably purchased the data from Opta. When the Premier League fantasy football app tells you that a striker has taken a certain number of shots over the course of the season, this stat will probably have been bought off Opta. When a newspaper match report references the average possession of a particular team in their last few matches, this information will probably have been supplied by Opta. Most football performance stats which filter through to the public will probably have been originally collected by one of Opta's many analysts.

Opta Sports was founded in the 1990s by a group of management consultants aiming to create a player performance index in football. They began collecting data on every player in the English top flight with the aim of producing a reliable and informative index of each of these players' performances. Initially, the aim was to increase the brand of their company by gaining exposure through media outlets such as Sky Sports and *The Observer* newspaper. However, they soon discovered that the data they were collecting was far more valuable than the exposure they were gaining. Media outlets were desperate to buy stats from them, as were English football clubs themselves. The data revolution of football had truly begun.

Initially, the methods that Opta used to collect their data were nothing special. Like Reep, they had to make do with a pen and paper. The stats that they were recording were as basic as shots, saves and passes. The matches were recorded on a video camera, the footage of which would be stopped and started for hours by the analysts as they logged the data. Recent technological advancements mean that Opta's analysts now have more sophisticated means of collecting the stats. Computers have replaced notepads. This has allowed Opta to log an increasing number of events. The amount of actions which take place in each game tend to range between 3,000 and 4,000. Opta collect a huge amount of information; every pass, dual, interception, cross, save. Every touch which happens during the course of a match is recorded by the company. In recent years, Opta have also begun collecting Expected Goals data.

Opta's data resources are vast. They can tell you the aerial abilities of any central defender, the passing percentage of any midfielder or the shooting accuracy of any forward. Opta possess a huge amount of information, and in a sport where predictive success is both hard to achieve and vital to success, information is power.

THE HISTORY OF TSR

Opta have collected data on events such as shots, passes and interceptions for decades. Access to this information has changed the way the sport is analysed. However, as we will study in the coming sections, this information is more *descriptive* than *predictive*. These events are good at describing what has happened, but does not tell us much about what is going to happen in the future. An example of a descriptive statistic is something like, "*Everton have not dropped out of the Premier League since its formation in 1992*". Whilst this stat may be interesting, it does not tell us anything about how Everton will perform in the coming years. A statement such as, "*Manchester City have amassed the most passes of any team this season*", is both descriptive and predictive. We know that there is some correlation between the number of passes a team makes and their success, but this analysis is too shallow to draw any meaningful conclusions about Man City's future performance. The most predictive stat is Expected Goals data – xG gives the most profound insight into how well a team has performed, and therefore how well they are likely to perform in the future. Pundits, analysts and managers should be more interested in predictive data than descriptive data, as predictive data gives a better indication of future performance.

Football started by simply looking at the number of goals that teams scored. This the most basic statistic there is. The more goals a team scores, and the fewer they concede, the more matches they will win. Reep's innovation was to look deeper into the sport and measure the number of passes teams were making. Following this, statisticians began clocking the number of shots that teams were taking. This seems natural; generally speaking, the more shots a team has, the more goals they are likely to score. Early analysts found a strong correlation between the number of shots a team were taking and the number of points they were picking up over the course of the season.

Football's interest in using shots as a statistic stemmed from the sport of hockey. The two sports are similar in some respects. In both, two teams launch a series of attacks with the aim of scoring in the opposition's goal. However, in hockey the amount of shots which a team has serves as a reliable measure of their possession. An analyst can reliably conclude that a team who is having a lot of shots is having a lot of possession of the puck. In football, this is less true. Leicester City's 2015/16 Premier League winning team are a good example of a side who had minimal possession, but managed to create lots of scoring opportunities due to their counter-attacking approach. The correlation between shots and possession is a lot looser in football than it is in hockey. In hockey, the number of shots a team takes is incredibly *predictive*, whereas in football it is more *descriptive*.

The Expected Goals method is the most powerful metric that can be used to analyse teams and players. But before Expected Goals, there was something called Total Shots Rate (TSR). It will be useful to study how TSR advanced the football analytics evolution, how it served as the precursor to xG, but why it ultimately falls short as a predictive metric.

Football analysts have long since recognised the correlation between the number of shots a team takes and the success of that team. A key metric for testing this hypothesis is the Total Shots Rate (TSR) of a team. TSR follows a simple formula, but allows analysts a decent indicator of a team's future performance. The formula for TSR is as follows:

Total Shots Rate = Shots For / (Shots For + Shots Against)

The TSR of a team is the number of shots which they take in a match, divided by the total number of shots that took place. Thus, a team who takes any number of shots without reply from the opposition can be assigned a TSR of 1.0. A team who has six shots, but concedes four attempts, will carry a TSR of 0.6 (six divided by ten). If the number of shots of both teams are equal, then they will both hold a TSR of 0.5. Here is the TSR of both sides if we plug the data from the example match we used in the first chapter:

If Manchester City had 2 and Arsenal had 6 shots,

*Man City TSR = 2 / (2 + 6) = 2 / 8 = **0.25***

*Arsenal TSR = 6 / (2 + 6) = 6 / 8 = **0.75***

Arsenal's TSR is a large 0.75, whilst Man City's is just 0.25. The TSR of both sides is always 1.0 when added together, and the average of the two TSR totals is always 0.5. This is because, every time a shot is taken by one team, the other team concedes a shot. There is perfect parity between the two figures.

TSR is a strong indicator for the success of a team. James Grayson, the analyst who first came up with the formula for TSR, has emphasised the correlation between the metric and a team's position in the league. He took a sample of Premier League teams from 2000-2012 and compared their TSR to the amount of points they collected over the course of a season. The correlation that he found was incredibly strong. In fact, no side that has been relegated from the Premier League has ever scored above 0.52 TSR. This means that a team who are taking more shots than the opposition on average per match can be almost completely confident that they won't get relegated. Conversely, only one team in the sample achieved a top four spot without scoring above 0.5 TSR. This team was Everton in 2004/05, who managed to obtain fourth spot with an average 0.45 TSR. Generally speaking, the higher a team's TSR, the more points they scored in a season.

Figure 3-1: Correlation Between TSR and Points (Premier League, 2000-2012)

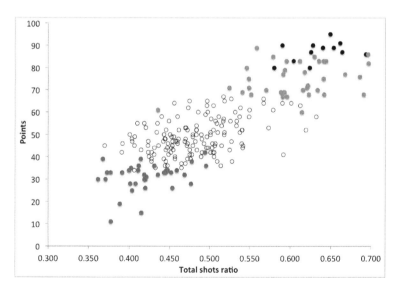

Total Shots Rate is a good indicator of success, but it does have large drawbacks. The problem with the formula is that it treats all shots equally. In football, some chances are going to be a lot easier to score than others. An effort from two yards out has a higher probability of hitting the back of the net than a shot from forty yards out. TSR doesn't take into account the quality of shots, only the quantity.

The metric would work perfectly if all teams created an equal amount of good chances as poor chances. However, it is unrealistic to assume that the distribution of low quality shots to high quality shots is equal for all teams. Arsenal, for example, have gained a reputation over recent years for passing the ball to death. The Gunners are often accused of "over-playing" and are encouraged by their fans to take more shots. Whilst Arsenal's lack of attempts at goal may not see them rank too favourably on the TSR scale, the shots that they *do* take tend to be of very high quality. They work themselves into good positions in order to make it easier to score when they do shoot. Other teams take the opposite approach and choose to shoot on sight. They take lots of long range shots in the hope that a barrage on the opposition goalkeeper will end in a goal or two. Whilst these teams will rank highly in TSR, they will not necessarily be scoring more goals. Each one of their shots will only have a low probability of scoring.

The Total Shots Rate was good, but football needed a way of accounting for the *quality* of shots being taken. This is where Expected Goals stepped in and provided an answer.

THE HISTORY OF EXPECTED GOALS

In April 2012, an analyst called Sam Green posted a blog article on the OptaPro forum (an online forum where analysts can post interesting statistical discoveries) introducing the idea that shot quality might be just as important as shot quantity. In other words, a team who are creating fewer chances but from a closer range might be better than a team who are taking lots of speculative long shots. The article also studied, albeit at a fairly primitive level, how a metric called Expected Goals might help value individual players. Thus, with an inconspicuous blog post, the foundations of the Expected Goals method were laid.

The Expected Goals method began to feature on an increasing number of niche online blogs. Amateur analysts developed the method after taking inspiration from similar means of analysis which existed in ice hockey. However, the football analytics community makes up a tiny fraction of the online content surrounding football, meaning that very few people were aware of xG until very recently.

In the Summer of 2013, Ted Knutson founded a website called Statsbomb. Knutson, having worked in sports betting for several years, realised that there was a lot of good football analytics content beginning to appear online. The problem was that this content was scattered all over the web. Statsbomb's intention was to serve as a hub for the football analytics community, where "fanalysts" (fans who take interest in the statistical side of sport) could write articles on various teams, players and tactics, using data to justify their beliefs. Knutson stated in his first post that Statsbomb was "going to be a place for analysts to publish their work on a website with a bigger, more regular traffic footprint than their personal blog". As with many bloggers in the early days of the modern football analytics movement, Knutson's work soon got noticed.

In 2014, Knutson was hired by Smartodds as the Head of Football Analytics. Smartodds are a betting consultancy who collect data, analyse it and sell their findings to professional gamblers. These high-rolling clients use the company's data to make millions in the betting markets. Smartodds is owned by Matthew Benham, who also owns Championship club Brentford FC. As well as selling Smartodds' data to pro gamblers, Benham also uses it to scout players for the West London outfit, allowing them to punch well above their financial weight. More on that later on.

Knutson oversaw the recruitment and data-driven decision-making of Brentford. He played a large role in the club's early success in the Championship, but Benham's ruthless modernisation of his analytics team meant that Knutson was soon found surplus to requirements.

In 2016, Knutson left Smartodds, but a year later expanded Statsbomb from an online resource for data into Statsbomb Services – his own data consultancy. Where Opta sell their data to the media and Smartodds sell their data to professional gamblers, Knutson's target market was professional football clubs. Knutson stated that his goal was to "produce the best possible analytic toolset for clubs to use in player recruitment, team analysis and opposition scouting". Statsbomb claim to have clients in the German Bundesliga, Major League Soccer, EFL Championship and the Europa League.

The career of Ted Knutson serves as a useful case study with which we can track the progression of the Expected Goals method. The first to catch on were the betting syndicates and gambling consultancies. These entities can only survive if they have an edge over the competition. Their livelihoods depend on curating the most intelligent models, collecting the most profound data and delivering the smartest means of analysis. Smartodds are industry leaders when it comes to the gambling consultancy field. Their ground-breaking means of collecting and analysing Expected Goals data has led them to unparalleled success in predicting the outcome of sporting fixtures.

Since Knutsen's arrival as Head of Football Analytics at Smartodds back in 2014, an increasing number of football clubs have adopted the Expected Goals method as a more intelligent means of scouting players and profiling upcoming opposition, as well as measuring their own team's performance. Obviously, professional clubs are keen to keep their scouting tools under wraps in order to maintain whatever edge they might have over their opposition. Thus, very few people can be certain of the exact methods that the top clubs use to identify talent in the market. However, there is evidence that the Expected Goals method is having an increasing impact in the decision-making of teams.

Arsène Wenger has been at the forefront of this philosophical shift within the sport. In 2012, the ex-Arsenal manager purchased StatDNA, a US-based analytical company. StatDNA was one of the fastest growing data collection organisations, offering expert analysis on sporting performance. The measly sum of £2m that Arsenal paid for the company is just a drop in the ocean for a club of their size. Arsenal and Brentford are currently the only two English Football League sides to own their own, personal analytics companies; StatDNA and Smartodds. This allows these two clubs to collect whatever type of data they want – they have compiled two of the most comprehensive and profound Expected Goals databases in existence. It also gives them an edge over other clubs, who have to purchase data for hefty premiums from companies such as Prozone and Opta.

So, the Expected Goals method spread quickly through the online football analytics community in 2012. Betting syndicates and professional gamblers quickly caught on, utilising the revolutionary metric to make millions. Professional football clubs were the next in line to harness the power of Expected Goals. Brentford were the main trailblazers, and are still reaping the rewards of several bargain signings made over the last few years. Other clubs have since caught on, and have implemented xG into their own scouting methods.

Each of these collectives (betting syndicates, professional clubs and football analysts) all have one thing in common: *they seek to maintain an edge over their competition.* Thus, the Expected Goals method has occupied a position far away from the limelight. Those who have understood its power from an early age have not looked to let others in on the secret. The Expected Goals method has remained in the shadows, hidden from the eyes of fans and the media.

However, at the beginning of the 2017/18 season, a huge step was taken by football media. Opta decided that there was finally enough interest in football analytics to present the Expected Goals methods to the general public. They started pushing xG to the media platforms who buy stats off them. As such, Sky Sports started offering occasional Expected Goals insight across their social media and during live broadcasts. In addition, the BBC's *Match of the Day* started showing the Expected Goals scoreline of each Premier League match after the highlights of each fixture.

In November 2017, the Expected Goals method received more media attention as Arsène Wenger cited the Expected Goals scoreline in the post-match interview following his Arsenal side's defeat at the hands of Manchester City. As we saw in Chapter 1, the Frenchman claimed that the xG data showed that the match was much tighter than the actual scoreline suggested. This was met with derision from Jeff Stelling and mainstream football media.

Despite this setback, the football analytics community had waited for over half a decade for xG to be openly endorsed by a meaningful figure within the sport. Although Wenger's StatDNA had been using the Expected Goals method at Arsenal for a while, he had not openly spoken about it before. His public commendation was significant because, for the first time, Wenger felt that xG was not a closely guarded secret. By revealing his faith in it, the Frenchman was also admitting that it no longer gave him a meaningful edge. Five years ago, Wenger would have never dreamed of disclosing that Arsenal use the stat to their advantage, but recent public interest meant that there was now no harm in freely discussing xG.

Google Trends is a useful tool for determining the popularity of any search term over a certain period of time. The site displays a week-by-week account of how many times the term has been searched, on a scale of zero to one hundred (one hundred being the term's most searches in a week, zero being the fewest). *Figure 3-1* shows the frequency with which the term 'Expected Goals' has been typed into google over the last five years.

Figure 3-1: "Expected Goals" Google Search Proclivity

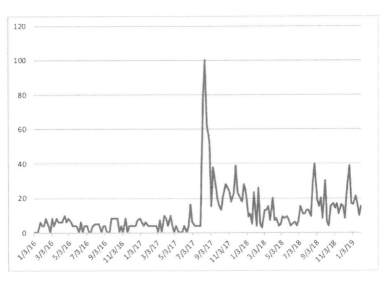

The large spike in the chart is the product of Jeff Stelling's famous rant. That very same week also saw the publishing of *The Football Code*, in which the Expected Goals method is heavily promoted. These two events in early September 2017 served as a catalyst for increased public interest in xG. Indeed, in the year and a half before Stelling's outburst, the average rating that Google attributes to the proclivity of the search term was 4.22. In the year and a half period after the Soccer Saturday publicly criticised the stat, ranging from early September 2017 to January 2019, the average rating was 18.6. Interest in Expected Goals has increased nearly five-fold.

So far, we have broadly looked at the history of football analytics and how the Expected Goals method has risen to prominence. Let us now turn our attention more specifically to how we can use the metric to answer some of football's toughest questions. How can we accurately measure the performance of teams? Who is the best player in the world? Can the average punter use Expected Goals to beat the bookmakers? And can clubs use xG to consistently identify and sign hidden gems?

4

EXPECTED VALUE

Can Mathematics Help You Win the Lottery?

WINNING THE LOTTERY

The Expected Goals method is founded on a mathematical principle known as Expected Value (EV). Expected Value can tell us the worth of a lottery ticket, the worth of a bet or the worth of a shot in football. It is utilised in almost every financial realm and is an incredibly important concept to comprehend when making predictions. An understanding of Expected Value is useful when studying the Expected Goals method.

The Expected Value of a variable is the long-run average value of repetitions of the experiment it represents. This sounds more complicated than it is. For instance, the Expected Value of a roll of a normal six-sided dice is 3.5, because this is the average of all the numbers which come up after a large number of rolls. Of course, it is impossible for us to roll a 3.5, but this is the average value that we would expect to come up if we rolled our dice, say, one million times. Likewise, the average person might expect to own 4.5 cars over the course of their lifetime. Obviously, it is impossible for anyone to own 4.5 cars, as it is impossible to break whole vehicles down into fractions. This figure simply reflects how many cars the average person might *expect* to own.

Expected Value is used frequently in financial settings. For example, if you wanted to work out whether or not to purchase a lottery ticket, you could work out the amount of money that you could expect to make back from it. To do this, you need information on how much money you stand to win and also the probability of you actually winning. Suppose that a lottery is selling one thousand tickets for £2 each. Only one ticket can win the jackpot, which is set at £1,500. You want to work out whether it is worthwhile investing £2 of your money on a ticket. Expected Value can help you do this, as it will tell you how much money you can expect the ticket to win over the long run.

The equation for working out Expected Value is simple. All you have to do is multiply the probability of each outcome occurring by the amount of money that you would make if it did occur, before adding all of these outcomes together. For example, in the lottery ticket example above there are only two possible outcomes: either you win the £1,500 jackpot or you don't. Thus, in order to work out the Expected Value of a lottery ticket we must carry out the following equation:

(Chance of winning x Winning amount) + (Chance of losing + Losing amount)

(1/1000 x £1,500) + (999/1000 x £0) = Expected Value of ticket

£1.50 + £0 = ***£1.50***

Using this simple equation, we can work out that the Expected Value of a ticket for this lottery is £1.50. *This is what the lottery ticket is worth.* If we entered this lottery on hundreds of thousands of occasions, we would expect to make back an average of £1.50 each time. (Remember, just as we cannot actually own 4.5 cars in our lifetime, we cannot actually win £1.50 on any occasion. This is simply the amount that we can expect to win each time over the long run). Seeing as we know that the value of each ticket for this lottery is £1.50, we can now decide whether or not to purchase one. Clearly, paying £2 for a ticket that is only worth £1.50 is a bad idea. If someone offered to swap their pen worth £1.50 in exchange for your pen worth £2, you wouldn't take the deal. When there is a negative Expected Value, as in our lottery example, you should never stake your involvement.

However, if someone offered you the same lottery ticket for £1, you should take the deal. Clearly, buying a ticket with an Expected Value of £1.50 for a cheaper price is good business.

The equation for Expected Value can also help us when there are more than two outcomes possible. Our prior example was simple; of the one thousand people who enter the lottery, one person wins the jackpot and nine-hundred and ninety-nine people walked away empty-handed. What happens when we introduce a couple more possible outcomes? Suppose that the lottery still sold one thousand tickets at £2 each, but this time the prize for the winning ticket is £500, the second-place and third-place tickets win £300 and the fourth-placed, fifth placed and sixth placed tickets win £100. Now there are four different outcomes possible: you win £500, you win £300, you win £100 or you win nothing. Each of these outcomes also have a different probability of occurring. The equation remains inherently the same, just with the updated variables:

(Chance of first-placed ticket x First-placed winnings) + (Chance of second or third-placed ticket x Second or third-placed winnings) + (Chance of fourth, fifth or sixth-placed ticket x Fourth, fifth or sixth-placed winnings)

(1/1000 x £500) + (2/1000 x £300) + (3/1000 x £100) = Expected Value

£0.5 + £0.6 + £0.3 = **£1.40**

The Expected Value of a ticket for this particular lottery is £1.40. Seeing that one of the one thousand tickets will win £500, two of the one thousand tickets will win £300, three of the one thousand tickets will win £100 and nine-hundred and ninety-four tickets will win nothing, we could expect each random ticket to be worth £1.40 before the draw is made. Again, this means that each ticket offers us negative value when they are being priced at £2. If each ticket only cost £1, there would a positive expectation and it would be worth investing your money.

A strong grasp of Expected Value is crucial to success in any financial industry. Bookmakers, casinos, lotteries and mutual fund managers all make fortunes by offering negative Expected Value deals to unassuming customers. Each bet placed at a bookmaker, each lottery ticket purchased at a corner shop and each stake wagered at a casino tends to have negative expectation. Over the long run, we will always lose money when dealing with these institutions. Bettors and gamblers are essentially buying products for less money that they are worth. They are paying £2 for commodities worth £1.50.

"NEXT ROUND'S ON EV"

I was once in a bar with some friends when someone proposed that we play "Card Roulette". In a game of Card Roulette, everyone in the group gives their debit card to the bartender, who randomly picks one card to pay for the entire round of drinks. Some of the group opted out, worried they would have to pay for the entirety of the hefty bill. Others were keen to take part, focusing on the likelihood of obtaining free drinks. To make my decision, I quickly worked out the Expected Value of partaking in the game.

There were six of us each wanting £8 worth of drinks. This meant that the unlucky individual who lost the game would have to pay for £48 worth of drinks (a loss of £40 because they still got to drink the £8 worth of alcohol that they spent on themselves), whilst the five who won would be gifted £8 worth of drinks for free. Here was the equation which needed working out:

(Chance of my card being drawn x Losses) + (Chance of my card not being drawn x Winnings)

(1/6 x -£40) + (5/6 x £8) = Expected Value

-£6.67 + £6.67 = £0

The Expected Value of entering the wager was £0. This makes sense when you think about it: when each individual has an equal chance of winning the same amount of drink, there is neither a negative nor positive expectation to be obtained. Over the long run, entering into the game would pay out the same amount as buying drinks for yourself. I decided that the social aspect of taking part tipped the decision in favour of placing my stake in the wager. On that particular occasion, the reader will be pleased to learn that the bartender did not select my card and I got £8 worth of drinks paid for by an unlucky friend.

There is a caveat to the game of Card Roulette. The Expected Value of entering the game is only £0 if you assume that the bartender is picking a card completely at random. One particular friend of mine refuses to play anymore, because his bright orange debit card was getting picked far more frequently by various bartenders than the rest of the group's dark green cards. If for some reason your card is consistently getting picked more often than the rest of the group's cards, then the Expected Value of your involvement in the game might drop below £0. If this is the case, you would not be getting value for money.

EVALUATING SHOTS IN FOOTBALL

Expected Value can also be used to evaluate the shots which take place in a football match. Fortunately, the formula for calculating the Expected Value of an attempt at goal could not be easier. Because goals are always worth one score in football (as opposed to sports like rugby and cricket, where a try is worth five scores and hitting the ball over the boundary is worth either four or six scores), the equation is incredibly simple. To work out the Expected Value of a shot (the xG), you

simply have to multiply the probability of the shot resulting in a goal by one. For example, penalties hit the back
of the net roughly 72% of the time. Thus, the following
equation reveals the Expected Value of a penalty:

(Chance of penalty being scored x Points for a goal)
+ (Chance of penalty being missed + Points for a
miss) = Expected Value (xG)

(0.72 x 1) + (0.28 x 0) = xG

*0.72 + 0 = **0.72(xG)***

In football, it is not even necessary to do this working
out. Because goals are worth one score, the Expected
Goals value of each shot is simply the decimal probability that the attempt will result in a goal. As we have seen,
the probability assigned to each effort on goal hitting
the back of the net depends on several variables: the position on the pitch where the shot takes place, whether it
is on the shooter's strong foot, the type of assist for the
shot, and so on and so forth.

It is not absolutely necessary to understand the inner
workings of Expected Value in order to comprehend
and appreciate the usefulness of the Expected Goals
method. However, hopefully you will agree that is interesting to understand the simple mathematic principle

behind xG. EV can help us decide whether or not to by a lottery ticket, whether or not to play a game of Card Roulette and whether or not your striker should have had that attempt at goal.

5

MATCHDAY xG

Why Do Winners Win?

ARISTOTLE'S THREE UNITIES

In drama, three unities represent the Aristotelian theory of dramatic tragedy. There is the unity of place: the action of a play should exist in a single physical location. There is the unity of time: the action of a play should occur over the course of a limited timescale. There is the unity of action: a play should be defined by a series of principal actions.

The average football fan might not be familiar with the theatrical works of Aristotle. However, great similarities can be drawn between the Greek philosopher's theory on the three unities of tragedy and the ways in which football analysts have come to visually represent Expected Goals data.

The first type of graphic used by xG analysts represents the location of each shot which takes place in a match (the unity of place). The second type of graphic indicates the timescale of the match from an xG standpoint (the unity of time). Finally, the third type of graphic outlines each individual Expected Goal value amassed by each team over the course of ninety minutes (the unity of action).

It is useful to collect Expected Goals data, but presenting the data in a way which tells a story is equally as important (especially for media companies who are looking to engage the ordinary football fan). The following three types of visualisation allows xG data to be easily digested.

THE UNITY OF PLACE: xG MAPS

Put yourself into the mind of the analyst sat at his desk on a Saturday afternoon. A match has just taken place which you are tasked with analysing. You want to assess the performance of both the teams using xG. For this purpose, let's take a real life match as a case study to outline the utility of the Expected Goals method. This game took place between Manchester City and Liverpool on 3rd January 2019. The teams were locked in a two-horse race for the Premier League title and the match turned out to be extremely significant. Manchester City triumphed by two goals to one, giving their title hopes an enormous boost.

When analysing the xG for a single match of football, there are several useful graphics that can be used to present the data. The most informative of which is an Expected Goals Map, which offers a bird-eye-view of the field of play. Each shot which takes place is represented by a dot in the location from which it was taken. The size of the dot indicates the Expected Goals value of the shot: the larger the value of the shot, the larger the volume of the dot representing it.

*Figure 5-1: Expected Goals Map for Manchester
City v Liverpool (03/01/19)*

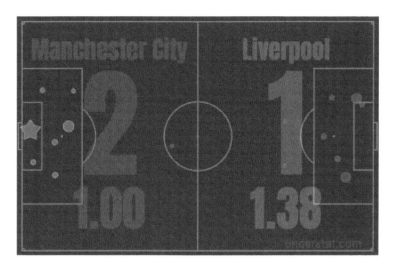

Consider *Figure 5-1*, the Expected Goals Map for
the Manchester City v Liverpool match according to
Understat.com. This website is a fantastic resource which
supplies Expected Goals statistics on teams and players
across the top five European leagues.

The first thing to note is the Expected Goals
scoreline of the match: Man City scored 1.00(xG) and
Liverpool scored 1.38(xG). This already gives us a large
amount of information. It indicates that there wasn't a
great deal of goalmouth action, but that the visitors narrowly outperformed the hosts.

Studying the Expected Goals Map in greater depths allows us to see exactly how the major chances in the game played out. The scoring was opened in the 39th minute by Sergio Aguero, whose left-footed shot from a tight angle carried a value of just 0.05(xG) – reflecting the fact that the shot would be scored one in every twenty attempts it was taken.[2] This shot is represented by the small star inside the six-yard box on the right-hand side of the graphic. The second goal of the match was scored in the 63rd minute by Roberto Firmino, whose close-range header carried a weight of 0.62(xG). This attempt is represented by the large star inside Man City's six-yard box on the left-hand side of the graphic. (You might argue that the close-range nature of the chance would render its value higher, but remember that headers are much harder to convert than normal shots). Despite Liverpool drawing level, Man City snatched the win when Leroy Sané slotted home in the 71st minute. This shot, worth 0.06(xG), is signified by the small star level with the penalty spot inside Liverpool's penalty area.

As indicated by the Expected Goals Map, there were other chances of note in this fixture. Sadio Mané hit

---

2 We have already studied how shots are assigned an Expected Goals value. In essence, analysts use a number of variables (location of shot, whether it was on the player's stronger foot, the positioning of defenders, the type of assist, etc.) in order to calculate the probability of it resulting in a goal. Opta's model is founded on data from hundreds of thousands of past shots from across various leagues.

the post in the 17th minute with a shot worth 0.37(xG), whilst Sergio Aguero and Bernardo Silva missed chances worth 0.3(xG) and 0.32(xG) respectively.

Clearly, this type of graphic offers a far greater indication of how the match played out than the data typically used in football media. *Figure 5-2* outlines how **BBC** Sport's stats detail the same match.

Figure 5-2: BBC Sport's Stats for Manchester City v Liverpool (03/01/2019)

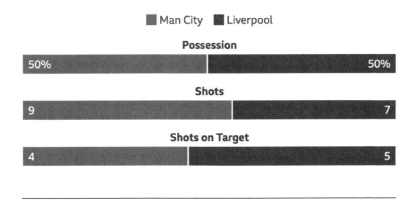

To be fair, the BBC's data does indicate the tightness of the match. Occasionally a match occurs in which one team has a lot of longshots and the other has a few close range chances. These matches are where Expected Goals really excels over the conventional stats of "Shots"

and "Shots on target", as xG offers profound insight into the *quality* of chances that each team created.

Still, the BBC's data indicates that Man City took two more shots than Liverpool. Anyone reading these stats might be forgiven for thinking that the hosts performed better than the visitors. However, in reality, the Expected Goals Map reveals that Man City created very few large chances. In addition, their two goals came from low danger situations (the xG values for Aguero's first half goal and Sané's winner add up to just 0.11(xG)). We can see that Liverpool were actually the better side, outperforming their opposition by 0.34(xG) in total.

Expected Goals Maps have become popular because of their naturalness. Football fans intuitively base their judgement on who should have won a game on the chances that each team created. An Expected Goals Map clearly shows the quantity, quality and locations of each shot.

The Manchester City v Liverpool example tells us that the hosts were slightly lucky to win, but it was a close game which could have gone either way. However, football has a tendency to produce much less fair results. *Figure 5-3* represents a match in which the final score was incredibly unreflective of the quality of the two sides.

Figure 5-3: Expected Goals Map for Chelsea v Leicester (22/12/18)

This match took place between Chelsea and Leicester at Stamford Bridge just a few weeks before the Man City v Liverpool clash. The Blues dominated, but were defeated by a Jamie Vardy goal early in the second half. Based on the chances they created, Chelsea amassed 2.40(xG) and Leicester totaled 0.46(xG).

This match perfectly demonstrates why luck plays such a large role in football. The low-scoring nature of the game means that bad teams regularly beat good teams. Chelsea generated five times the amount of xG as Leicester, yet still came away with no points. Studying the Expected Goals Map, one can see that Chelsea created a large volume of high quality chances inside the visitors' penalty area and six-yard box. However, on that particular day, the hosts were unable to convert any of these shots. Meanwhile, Leicester were restricted to only a handful of long shots and low quality opportunities. However, as fate would have it, one of these efforts found its way to the back of the net.

Chelsea fans might have criticised their team after the Leicester result. However, the xG data shows that *their team actually played well*. The Blues created a lot of chances and conceded very few chances. They were simply unlucky. If they were to maintain such performance levels throughout the season, their luck would eventually even out.

Matches of this nature occur every week. The infrequency with which goals are scored means that bad teams always have a chance of beating good teams. This creates excitement for the spectator, but creates a headache for the analyst trying to work out which teams are good and which are simply lucky. The use of Expected Goals Maps is one method through which a more accurate reading of the game can be gleaned.

THE UNITY OF TIME: xG TIMELINES

Expected Goals Maps provide a great snapshot of the location and quality of chances which each team created in a match. They neatly represent Aristotle's unity of place. However, they don't offer a clear image of the time in which these chances happened. A football match does not consist of a random cluster of attacks from either side. Anyone who has watched the sport will realise that, often, teams will exert spells of dominance over their opposition. The tide of a game ebbs and flows. Commentators often remark that "it is important to score whilst you are on top", because soon enough it will be your opponents' turn to enjoy a period of sustained pressure.

Figure 5-4 displays the Expected Goals Timeline for a match which took place between Brentford and Derby County in April 2019. The match served as a brilliant advertisement for Championship football, with the hosts equalising on three separate occasions in a fiercely contested three-all draw. The ebb and flow of the match is clearly demonstrated by Ben Mayhew's Expected Goals Timeline. Mayhew has made a name for himself in the football analytics community by producing such graphics for English Football League matches.

Figure 5-4: Expected Goals Timeline for
Brentford v Derby (06/04/2019)

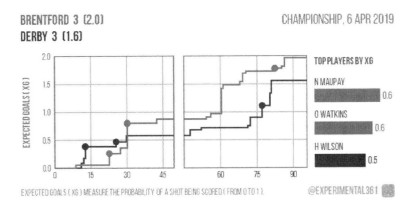

Once again, the first thing we should take note of is the Expected Goals scoreline from the game. Brentford amassed 2.0(xG), whilst Derby created enough chances to warrant 1.6(xG). Thus, the hosts outperformed their visitors. In actuality, both teams outperformed their Expected Goals totals by scoring three goals apiece. Another thing to recognise is the large combined xG total of the two teams – 3.6(xG) – which tells us that there was a lot of goalmouth action. Instantly, an analyst can observe that this was an open match in which both teams attacked wholeheartedly.

Turning our attention to the timeline itself, most of the features are fairly self-explanatory. On the horizontal axis, we have the minute of the match (from 0 to 95). On the vertical axis, we have the cumulative Expected Goals total for either team. Thus, each time either side takes a shot, the line representing them increases by the xG value of the attempt. For instance, the first attempt of the game took place by Brentford in the 8th minute and was worth 0.04(xG). Thus, their line moves above Derby's at this point in the game.

A shot which results in a goal is signified to have a dot at the top of it. The first goal in this match was scored by Derby in the 13th minute, from a shot which was worth 0.32(xG). This point is clearly noticeable in the graphic.

Expected Goals Timelines serve a number of useful purposes.

Primarily, the graphic clearly indicates the periods in a game in which each team were dominant. The Expected Goals Timeline gives analysts a unique insight into the spells of pressure which each side endured during the match. The graphic for the match between Brentford and Derby demonstrates how a game can ebb and flow. After an entertaining first half an hour, the game died down a bit until the hour mark. Brentford seized control and created a series of openings between the 60th and 70th minute, after which the game swung back in Derby's favour. Clearly, there were spells when either time was on top. Additionally, there were spells when the game was more open and spells when the game was more closed up.

Expected Goals Timelines also offer a greater insight into when chances were missed, as well as how great those chances were. For instance, Brentford missed an opportunity worth 0.48(xG) in the 61st minute of the match. This huge chance occurred in the middle of Brentford's period of extensive pressure between the 55th and 72nd minute, offering the Bees a great opportunity to take the lead. The home fans might regretfully wonder how the match would have progressed had this chance been scored.

Generally, Expected Goals Timelines offer a useful snapshot of how a match was played out. At what point were there big chances? When did each team have to endure spells of pressure? Was the game open throughout? Were there any periods where the sides struggle to create chances?

Figure 5-5 through *Figure 5-8* show various matches which occurred on 27th April 2019 throughout the football league. Some scorelines were more fair then others. Some matches were more open than others. Each Expected Goals Timeline tells a different story.

JAMES TIPPETT

Figure 5-5: Expected Goals Timeline for Millwall v Stoke (27/04/2019)

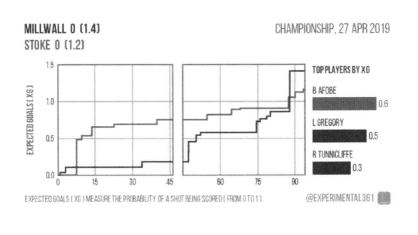

Figure 5-6: Expected Goals Timeline for
Accrington v Plymouth (27/04/2019)

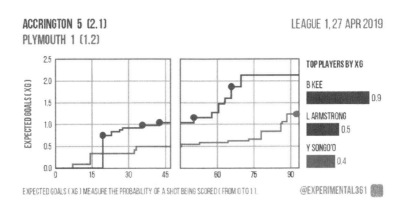

Figure 5-7: Expected Goals Timeline for QPR v Nottingham Forest (27/04/2019)

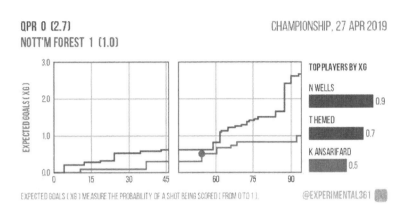

Figure 5-8: Expected Goals Timeline for Fleetwood v Bristol Rovers (27/04/2019)

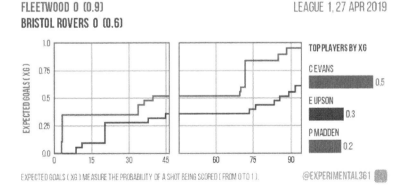

THE UNITY OF ACTION: xG LIVE UPDATES

Expected Goals Maps allow an insight into the locations from which each team created scoring opportunities over the course of a match, adhering to Aristotle's unity of place. Expected Goals Timelines offer insight into when each team created their opportunities, adhering to Aristotle's unity of time. The third unity in which Expected Goals data can be presented is slightly more basic.

Expected Goals Live Updates are list-like summations of the xG accumulated by either team through a match. *Figure 5-9* represents the xG Live Updates for the fixture between Brentford and Derby in April 2019. Although less visually stimulating than an Expected Goals Map or Expected Goals Timeline, the Expected Goals Live Updates does give you a decent impression on how the match was played out. The great advantage of this form of graphic is the precision with which it presents the data. We are able to glean the exact amount of xG that each team accumulated in the exact moment that the chance was created. More advanced xG Live Updates graphics can include the player who took the shot, the player who assisted the shot and a whole host of other data points which an analyst might be interested in.

Figure 5-9: Expected Goals Live Updates for
Brentford v Derby (06/04/2019)

Brentford	Time	Derby
0.02	07:38	
	09:26	0.09
	10:11	0.14
	12:56	0.26
0.18	22:45	
	26:42	0.07
0.06	28:33	
	30:14	0.03
0.38	30:49	
0.09	42:00	
	47:03	0.12
	51:26	0.06
0.04	56:42	
0.07	58:51	
0.48	60:14	
0.08	60:58	
0.02	67:34	
0.23	68:16	
0.06	69:54	
	70:35	0.07
	71:19	0.13
	77:48	0.19
	80:57	0.22
	81:41	0.16
0.07	83:27	
0.03	85:28	
0.2	86:52	

The Expected Goals method is enhanced when we use visually stimulating and informative graphics to present the data. This is the stumbling block at which media companies have fallen. Sky Sports and BBC Sport have successfully adopted xG as a metric with which to measure teams and players. However, they have failed to present their audiences with any of the graphics outlined in this chapter. The media companies have simply quoted the xG scorelines of matches and the accumulated Expected Goals totals of players throughout a season. These statistics are extremely useful, but are not entirely engaging. The average fan is more likely to respond to a visual graphic, such as an Expected Goals Map or Expected Goals Timeline. This is the next big step which media companies need to take.

Hopefully the reader now has a greater understanding of how Expected Goals can help us more accurately assess the performance level of teams, how it can tell us which sides are more deserving of winning and how we can present xG data visually through a series of graphics. Expected Goals Maps, Expected Goals Timelines and Expected Goals Live Updates allow us a profound insight into the nature of how matches played out.

Now let's turn our attention away from the collective, and towards the individual. How can we use the Expected Goals method to measure the performance of players?

6

PLAYER xG

Who is the Best Player in the World?

THE GREATEST ANALYTICAL CHALLENGE

Before we study how the Expected Goals method can help us assess the ability of players, we must recognise the challenges associated with using data to recognise individual talent. Fans, managers and analysts have long since struggled to measure the skill of players. This challenge is part of what makes football such an interesting sport. Millions of hours of human existence have been spent debating the ability of various footballers. Why should one player start over another? Which players should we put in our fantasy football teams? Who is the best player in the world? Such questions fuel football's relentless debate forums, social media presence and office conversation.

There are several reasons behind our struggle to assess players using data.

First of all, we must once again recognise the limitations placed on us by the lack of goals which occur in football. If the reader takes one thing away from this book, it should be an acknowledgement of the almighty role that luck plays in low-scoring sports such as football. Good teams often lose and bad teams often win. Such randomness easily echoes onto players. Good strikers often suffer goal droughts, whilst bad strikers often outperform their natural ability. Michu, Christian Benteke, Papiss Cisse and Roque Santa Cruz all serve as notable examples of footballers who benefitted (briefly) from the way goals randomly distribute themselves – these players all enjoyed one-off seasons of great over-performance. Conversely, some great players suffer at the hands of football randomness. Eden Hazard tallied a 14-, 16-, 12- and another 16-goal season in 2014/15, 2016/17, 2017/18 and 2018/19 respectively. However, many people forget the measly 4-goal campaign the Belgian endured during 2015/16. Data doesn't always tell the true story, making player analysis difficult.

And the randomness which affects individual player data is only half the problem. Most of the time we don't even know *what data we are meant to be looking at.* Players can be measured using a seemingly endless list of metrics. Pass completions, aerial duals, tackles, shots, shot accuracy, interceptions, touches, fouls, distance covered, etc. The list of data points goes on and on. How do we decipher which ones are more useful than others? And how does that translate into improving the performance level of the entire team?

Sometimes even our most basic intuitions turn out to be completely flawed. A decade or so ago, it was widely accepted that defensive ability was directly linked to how many tackles a defender made. This seems instinctive. The role of defenders is to prevent goals being conceded. You can prevent goals being conceded by making tackles. Therefore, the defenders who make the most tackles are clearly the best defenders. Right? Wrong. Nowadays, it is recognised that if a defender has to make a tackle, he has already made a mistake. The great Paolo Maldini, widely regarded as one of the greatest centre-backs of all time, averaged only 0.56 challenges per game during his career. The Italian's positioning and ability to read the game was so good that the man he was marking hardly ever saw the ball. Tackling was something Maldini used only as a last resort.

Whilst on the topic of defenders, we should acknowledge the differences in how attacking players and defensive players are analysed. It is much easier to collect data on forwards. This is because attacking is generally an individual enterprise, whilst defending is a collective responsibility. A *player* scores a goal; a *team* concedes a goal. When a player scores, makes an assist or completes a successful take on, this data is easily afforded to him. He tends to take all the credit. However, when a goal is conceded, the blame tends to fall on all of the defenders and the goalkeeper. The blame is distributed amongst several players, meaning it is hard to tell who is truly at fault.

The increased difficulty in using data to measure defensive performance rather than attacking performance is a double-edged sword. On the one hand, defenders who concede lots of goals are probably less likely to receive criticism than a striker who is not scoring goals (because it is easier to blame a striker for his individual failure than it is to blame a defender for the failure of his collective defensive unit). On the other hand, a striker who is performing well is more likely to win praise and accolades than a defender who is performing well (again, because it is easier to single out the striker than the defender). In fact, not a single defender or goalkeeper won the PFA Players' Player of the Year award between 2005 (John Terry) and 2019 (Virgil Van Dijk).

Perhaps our greatest foil in attempting to use data to measure individual ability is the dynamism of football. The twenty-two players on the field are constantly in motion. The action of one directly affects the action of another. Similarly, the ability of one directly affects the performance of another. It would be interesting to place a League Two midfielder in the best team in the world and see how much his game would be raised. Similarly, what would happen if you placed Lionel Messi in a League Two match? We will never know.

What we do know is that the dynamic nature of football makes it even harder to measure individual player performance using data. Sports such as baseball and cricket consist of a limited number of easily definable actions. In baseball, there is the pitch of the ball, the strike of the ball and the fielding of the ball. These actions can be easily recorded and scrutinised. In football, there are so many actions happening by so many agents at any one time that the data soon becomes overwhelming. Finding relevant, useful and insightful player stats is like finding a needle in a stack of broken needle parts.

But it is not good enough for us to admit defeat. Football's popularity lies in its unrelenting ability to produce drama, to produce enthralling narratives and to produce heroes and villains. Thus, we find imperfect ways of awarding talent. We annually honour a Player of the Season, a Team of the Year and prizes such as the Ballon D'or. There is no science to such merit distribution. There is no definitive right or wrong answer to who should obtain such accolades. It's based entirely on opinion. Who's to say what makes one nominee more deserving than another? And how do we choose where to assign value?

Should awards be distributed based on the number of goals players score? But then defenders get hard done by. Maybe it should be allocated based on the trophies an individual has won that season? But then good players in poor teams get let down. And who gets to decide these awards? No one can claim to have watched enough football to accurately assess the claim of every player. These interminable questions demonstrate the difficulty we face when attempting to define the individual skill of footballers.

To Shoot or Not to Shoot?

In the previous chapter, we studied how the Expected Goals method can be used to analyse the performance of teams. Each shot is awarded a percentage chance of hitting the back of the net based on a series of factors (location, type of assist, whether it was on the player's stronger foot, etc.). These "Shot Probabilities" can be translated into Expected Goal values – i.e. a shot with a 20% chance of scoring is worth 0.2(xG). This data can be used to assess which teams are creating the greatest quality of chances, providing a more accurate representation of their performance than their results will do. Adding up each team's xG Shot Probabilities will give you an Expected Goals scoreline for a match (i.e. Manchester City 1.00(xG) – 1.38(xG) Liverpool). But if we can use Expected Goals to measure the performance of teams, can we use the same method to measure the performance of players?

In 2018/19, Liverpool marginally missed out on the Premier League title to Manchester City. Their free-flowing brand of football was undoubtedly inspired by the ferocious attacking trio of Roberto Firmino, Mohamed Salah and Sadio Mané. For the purposes of explaining how xG can help us analyse individual performance, we are going to use the latter player as a case study.

Sadio Mané scored twenty-two goals in the thirty-six Premier League appearances that he made in 2018/19. He was joint winner of the Golden Boot alongside Salah and Pierre-Emerick Aubameyang. In total, Mané took eighty-seven shots over the course of the 3100 minutes in which he played. This data gives us a certain amount of information – for instance, the forward's conversion rate was an impressive 25.3% (22 goals from 87 shots). However, we are still left with several questions. What kind of chances were being presented to Mané? What kind of areas was he shooting from? Could we have expected him to score more goals based on the opportunities he had?

Figure 6-1: Sadio Mané's Shot Map (Premier League, 2018/19)

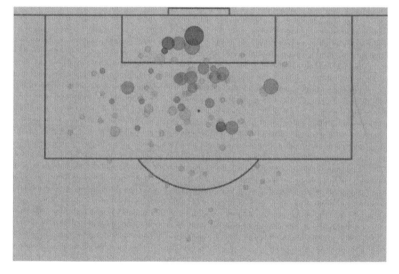

Figure 6-1 shows every shot that Sadio Mané took in the 2018/19 Premier League season, courtesy of *Understat. com*. As with the Expected Goals Maps we studied in the last chapter, the location of each dot represents the location of the attempt and the size of each dot represents its probability of resulting in a goal. For instance, the dot at the lowest point in the graphic represents a long-shot worth 0.02(xG) that Mané attempted during Liverpool's two-nil victory at the Cardiff City Stadium. The dot at the highest point in the map (the large dot situated centrally in the six-yard box, the closest distance from which Mané attempted a shot in 2018/19) represents a right-footed attempt worth 0.95(xG) taken during Liverpool's four-two victory over Burnley at Anfield.

Some things become immediately apparent. For instance, we can note that Mané's shots were mainly distributed to the left-hand side of the graphic. This makes sense, as the forward was usually deployed on the left side of an attacking three. Despite his position on the left-wing, Mané still managed a remarkable number of centrally positioned shots. More impressive still is the closeness to goal from which Mané's shots were attempted. An enormous proportion of his attempts were from central areas within the penalty area.

Figure 6-2: Anthony Martial's Shot Map
(Premier League, 2018/19)

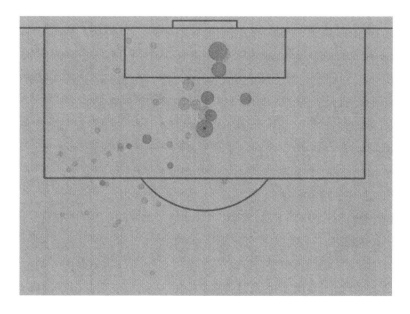

The true impressiveness of Mané's shot map is revealed when compared to that of another left-winger.
Figure 6-2 shows every shot that Anthony Martial took
during 2018/19. The Manchester United forward enjoyed a less fruitful campaign, although we should note
that Martial presents us with a smaller sample of data
than Mané. However, it is immediately apparent from

comparing the two shot maps that Martial struggled to get into the same areas as Mané. The Manchester United player took a plethora of shots from long distance on the left-hand side of the pitch – most of which were worth less than 0.05(xG). Consistently shooting from this distance is not a sustainable approach for a team looking to push for the title.

The Expected Goals method provides useful data, but that data still needs context in order to provide insight. For instance, we might question why Mané was able to get into more advanced positions than Martial. Was the Liverpool player better at beating men and creating space for himself in the area? Or was Mané aided by superior teammates who provided better assists for him and were better at working the ball close to goal? Finding the answers to these questions would provide deeper analysis, but I would suggest it was a combination of both factors.

My favourite player shot map, presented in *Figure 6-3*, is Andros Townsend's from the 2017/18 season. The Crystal Palace winger took an incredible sixty-two shots (just twenty-five short of Mané's total in 2018/19), but scored only two goals. Townsend's conversion rate was a measly 3%. Taking a quick glance at the player's shot map reveals why.

Figure 6-3: Andros Townsend's Shot Map (Premier League 2017/18)

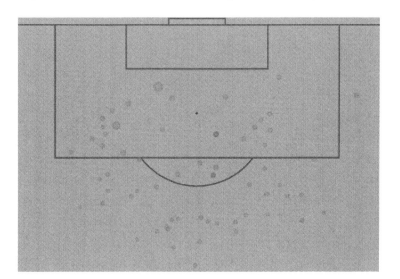

Recall how to calculate the Expected Goals scoreline of a match. The xG shot values of each side are added up – for instance, Man City 1.00(xG) – 1.38(xG) Liverpool. These totals reflect how many goals a team would have expected to score based on the quality of chances that they created. Adding up the xG shot values that a player has amassed over the course of a season will have the same effect. For example, Andros Townsend's sixty-two shots only amassed to a total of 3.11(xG). His average shot was worth 0.05(xG) – that's 3.11(xG) divided by 62 (shots). Meanwhile, the eighty-seven shots which Sadio

Mané took in 2018/19 amassed to a total of 16.76(xG). Thus, the Liverpool forward's average shot was worth 0.19(xG), reflecting the fact that he got into much better shooting positions.

An analyst with access to a player's Expected Goals data can carry out several different analyses of this kind. The study above is fairly shallow. Our conclusion that Sadio Mané is able to get into better scoring positions than Andros Townsend is one that we probably could have come to on our own.

However, it should be clear how this type of information can influence managers or coaches in tactical planning. Are their players getting into the right positions? Where are they being restricted? Which zones of the pitch are they finding it easiest to exploit? And conversely, what types of shots are they conceding? What kind of areas are the opposition getting into? Are there any key men to watch out for in upcoming opponents? The Expected Goals method is becoming increasingly influential in tactical planning of this kind. The key lesson to be learned from our own case study is that if Andros Townsend is in possession near the penalty area, he will probably shoot.

Is "Clinicalness" a Myth?

Adding up the shot values of every attempt that a player takes over the course of the season will give you their Expected Goals total. When you add up all the shots that Sadio Mané took in 2018/19 – from the unlikely 0.02(xG) long-range effort against Cardiff, to the sitter worth 0.95(xG) against Burnley – you get a total of 16.76(xG). This is how many goals you would have expected Mané to score over the course of the season.

The most obvious (and common) Expected Goals analysis which is carried out on players involves comparing their season-long xG total to the actual number of goals that they scored. Sadio Mané scored twenty-two goals in 2018/19 from a total of just 16.76(xG). This over-performance of 5.24(xG) was actually the largest positive difference in the Premier League that season. No other player outperformed their xG by such a large total. This data might prompt us to note Mané's clinical nature.

We have seen the utility in comparing the expected performance of teams to their actual performance. The Expected Goals method allows us to see which teams are creating the better chances, irrespective of whether or not those chances are converted. Thus, xG strips luck from results and allows us insight into who is actually playing better. *However, there is a crucial difference in how we intuitively use xG to analyse teams and players.*

If a team are creating lots of chances, but scoring few goals, we generally conclude that they have been unlucky. We assume that such a team's results will eventually begin to reflect their performance levels. And vice versa, a team who are scoring lots of goals from very few chances will eventually fall away in the league table. This logic is intuitive, and has been proven statistically. If a team's results are radically different from their Expected Goals scorelines, that team's performance level has been known to regress to the expected level sooner rather than later.

However, we seem to follow a different logical path when using the Expected Goals method to measure player performance. Sadio Mané outperformed his Expected Goals total by an incredible 5.24(xG) in 2018/19. But, rather than attributing this over-performance to luck (like we would do if a team were outperforming their xG), we tend to attribute it to the skill of the player. We would assume that Mané scored so many goals because of his superior finishing ability, his "clinical" nature.

This is one of the biggest problems that people have with the Expected Goals method. I have regularly been asked questions like: "If Cristiano Ronaldo and Glenn Murray take a shot from the same position, how can you give each shot the same chance of resulting in a goal? Surely Ronaldo is far more likely to convert than Murray?". Opta's Expected Goals model takes the average probability of a shot going in from a huge database of past shots. Therefore, the xG value they assign to each attempt reflects the probability that the *average* player would score from that situation. Surely the finishing quality of the player taking the shot will modify the chances of the attempt hitting the back of the net? Surely Cristiano Ronaldo is more likely to score when shooting from the same position as Glenn Murray?

This point is valid. However, I would offer the rebuttal that *finishing ability does not vary as much as we might be inclined to believe.* There are very few players who have consistently outperformed their Expected Goals output season upon season. In order to demonstrate this, let me present the xG data of one of history's greatest marksmen.

Figure 6-4 displays Cristiano Ronaldo's Expected Goals performance between 2015/16 and 2018/19. The Portuguese is widely regarded as one of the world's best finishers. The number of goals he has accumulated throughout his career is almost unparalleled. Ronaldo's goal-scoring prowess allowed him to win the Ballon D'or in 2016 and 2017 and come runner-up in 2018. As demonstrated in the figure, he consistently scored in excess of twenty goals over the course of these four campaigns.

Figure 6-4: Cristiano Ronaldo's Expected Goals Performance (2015-2019)

Season	Team	Apps	Minutes	Goals	xG	xG Dif
2018/19	Juventus	30	2602	21	22.87	+1.87
2017/18	Real Madrid	27	2304	26	27.01	+1.01
2016/17	Real Madrid	29	2546	25	25.41	+0.41
2015/16	Real Madrid	36	3186	35	35.59	+0.59

However, remarkably, *Cristiano Ronaldo actually underperformed his Expected Goals output in each of these four seasons.* Even in 2015/16, when accumulating a mammoth thirty-five goals for Real Madrid, Ronaldo's xG output stood at 35.59(xG). Ronaldo has consistently underperformed what would be expected of him in terms of finishing.

And if this doesn't convince you of the standardisation of finishing ability, let us look at a few other examples. Sadio Mané, the player who outperformed his Expected Goals data by the greatest quantity in the 2018/19 Premier League, underperformed in 2017/18 (scoring 10 goals from 11.52(xG)) and in 2015/16 (11 goals from 12.51(xG)).

Pierre-Emerick Aubameyang, joint Golden Boot winner with Mané in the 2018-19 campaign, scored his 22 goals from 23.55(xG). The average player would have expected to score more than the top scorer in the division (if presented with the exact same chances). In fact, Aubameyang himself has underperformed his Expected Goals in four of his last five seasons (2014/15, 2015/16, 2017/2018 and 2018/19).

These examples aren't exceptions to the rule. They are the rule. No player consistently outperforms his Expected Goals output season upon season. Whilst some players may seem more clinical than others, all professional strikers appear to possess roughly the same finishing prowess. I challenge the reader to search through *Understat*'s vast database of Expected Goals data and find any player who has outperformed his xG for five consecutive seasons. Not only is it impossible to find a player who consistently outperforms his scoring expectation, but the number of great players who regularly underperform their xG is astounding.

So, what can we make of all this?

First, we should recognise that what separates the top forwards is not finishing ability. Even the great Cristiano Ronaldo has actually scored fewer goals than the average forward would have been expected to from the exact same chances over the last four seasons. What makes Ronaldo a great player isn't his ability to finish chances, but his ability to create dangerous chances in the first place. His ability to dribble past players, get on the end of crosses, find space in the box and get to loose balls first has allowed him to consistently accumulate an extraordinarily high Expected Goals output each season. The same can be said for Mané and Aubameyang; they are set apart from lesser players by their supreme dribbling ability, rapid pace and exceptional reading of the game rather than by "clinicalness".

Second, we should recognise the impact that these players' teammates have on their performance. We studied earlier how attacking is seen as an individual enterprise, whilst defending is seen as the responsibility of the collective. A player scores a goal; a team concedes a goal. However, we should acknowledge the impact that high quality teammates can have on the performance of a forward. Ronaldo's high xG output has been aided by colleagues who create good chances for him.

This brings us neatly onto a metric which analyses the teammates of goal-scoring players: Expected Assists.

EXPECTED ASSISTS (xA)

The Expected Goals method can be used to assess the type of shots players are taking, the type of positions they are getting into, as well as being able to tell us how many times they could have been expected to hit the back of the net. It tells us that Sadio Mané has been able to get into extremely dangerous areas. Andros Townsend, less so.

This gives us valuable insight into the performance of strikers, but leaves out creative players who aren't taking a lot of shots. The Expected Goals method seems to bypass players such as midfielders and full-backs, who do not take a high enough quantity of efforts at goal to produce an xG sample size of any statistical significance. However, these players can be measured by a metric known as Expected Assists (xA).

Whilst Expected Goals measures the chance that a shot will end in a goal, Expected Assists measures the likelihood that a pass will end up becoming a primary assist. The value that an Expected Assists model gives to a pass is based on a variety of factors, most notably the finishing destination of the pass (a completed pass which finds a forward close to goal is more likely to result in an assist than one which finds the forward on the edge of the area) and also the type of pass (ground passes are more likely to be converted than crosses). The xA model is not reliant on a shot being taken. It credits *all passes*, regardless of whether or not they precede an attempt at goal.

Assists have been a popular measure of player output for some time, but they are not necessarily a fair reflection of the chances being created. For example, should a midfielder who plays a simple pass to a teammate who scores a thirty-yard screamer be accredited in the same way as a midfielder who plays a defence-splitting pass which allows for a striker to tap into the net? No, they shouldn't. Expected Assists provides a more profound insight into the creativity of players.

Importantly, the Expected Assists values that a player produces is not merely calculated by adding up the Expected Goals value of their key passes. A player produces an xA value with every pass he makes, irrespective of whether that pass results in a shot. This is important. Players should be accredited with the value their pass carries independently of what happens to the ball after the pass is completed. Indeed, every single pass which is made during a match of football is awarded an Expected Assist value – although most will carry an extremely low xA. When one centre-back passes to the other centre-back in his own half he will probably achieve about 0.0001(xA). However, a midfielder who feeds his striker in one-on-one with the goalkeeper might expect to be awarded about 0.4(xA) – indicating that the average forward would have a 40% chance of scoring from his pass.

The main benefit of using Expected Assists is that it assesses all creative players as if they were providing for the same quality of forward. Because Expected Assists models are developed from using a database of hundreds of thousands of shots, xA is awarded from the probability that the *average player* would score as a result of the pass. In reality, midfielders who play for poor teams are always likely to get less assists, because they have worse forwards playing in front of them. If you put any midfielder in the Stoke City team, he would get less assists than if he played in the Barcelona team. If he played for the Potters, the forwards ahead of him would be less pacey, less skillful and have worse movement, making it harder for him to accumulate assists.

For example, say you feed a perfect through-ball into a forward who is one-on-one with a defender. Clearly, the chances of a goal being scored from your pass is higher if Lionel Messi is the player bearing down on goal than if it is Glenn Murray. The former is much more likely to get around defenders than the latter. You have played the same pass in both situations, but clearly are more likely to be awarded with an assist if your teammate is

Messi. In fact, you might not have even had the chance to play the pass if you were playing with Murray, because your striker might not have provided the movement required for a pass to be played. (Note: I have nothing personal against Glenn Murray).

Midfielders who are playing with bad forwards will always get less assists than those playing with good forwards. The primary advantage of the Expected Assists method is that it standardises the quality of teammate for every creative player. It takes into account the *probability that the average forward would score as a result of each pass.*

Let's look at an example which can demonstrate the utility of Expected Assists. In 2018/19, Eden Hazard won the Premier League Playmaker award – the award for the player with the most assists in the league. The Belgian tallied a total of fifteen assists for Chelsea, marginally beating the fourteen assists which Ryan Fraser made for Bournemouth. The Blue was praised by many as the most creative player in the division. However, *Understat.com*'s Expected Assist model painted a completely different picture.

The Expected Assists model revealed that, based on the quality of Eden Hazard's passes, the Belgian would have expected to tally 11.57(xA) – 3.43 less than the actual amount of assists he achieved. Clearly, Hazard benefitted from the quality of teammates that he played alongside. He was playing in a world class Chelsea side, allowing him to tally more assists than his passes deserved.

Conversely, the Expected Assists model showed that Ryan Fraser's passes merited him 16.18(xA) – 2.18 more than the actual number of assists he achieved. Where Hazard's numbers where inflated by the quality of teammate surrounding him, Fraser's numbers were hampered. The average player would have scored 16.18 goals from the passes which Fraser made in the 2018/19 campaign. However, the Scots' below-par Bournemouth teammates were unable to convert the chances expected of them.

Figure 6-5 shows the players who amassed the highest xA totals in the 2018/19 Premier League season. When assessed on Expected Assists, Ryan Fraser's performance in the 2018/19 season saw him stand head and shoulders above the likes of Eden Hazard, Raheem Sterling, Mo Salah and David Silva. The underperformance of his teammates by 2.18 was bettered only by Mo Salah, whose teammates only scored eight goals from the 10.47(xA) that he provided for them (a difference of 2.47).

Figure 6-5: Players Ranked by xA Total (Premier League, 2018/19)

No.	Player	Team	Mins	Assists	xA	xA90
1	Ryan Fraser	Bournemouth	3185	14	16.18	0.46
2	Eden Hazard	Chelsea	2935	15	11.57	0.35
3	Raheem Sterling	Man City	2788	10	10.79	0.35
4	Mo Salah	Liverpool	3274	8	10.47	0.29
5	David Silva	Man City	2426	8	10.11	0.38
6	Bernardo Silva	Man City	2851	7	8.63	0.27
7	Leroy Sané	Man City	1866	10	8.10	0.39
8	Andy Robertson	Liverpool	3223	11	8.06	0.22
9	James Maddison	Leicester	2877	7	7.94	0.25
10	Christian Eriksen	Tottenham	2772	12	7.88	0.26

Another feature to note is Fraser's xA90 – the amount of Expected Assists he generated per ninety-minutes of playing time. The Scot accumulated an astounding 0.46(xA) per match. There was only one player in Europe's top five leagues who accumulated a higher xA90 than Ryan Fraser; Lionel Messi.

THE BEST PLAYER IN THE WORLD

I have never particularly enjoyed the debate over who is the best footballer in the world. There are too many uncontrolled variables for a proper comparison to take place. Every player plays in a different league against teams of varying quality. Every player plays in a different team with teammates of varying quality. Every player plays under a different manager, in a different position, in a different system. How could we possibly hope to account for all these factors?

However, when one consults the Expected Goals data, there is one player who stands out amongst the rest.

Before presenting the analysis, I should state that I have no particular allegiance towards Lionel Messi. I can acknowledge the beauty with which he plays football, but I don't worship the ground he walks on. In fact, I dislike the narrative that regularly surrounds him. For instance, after Liverpool's miraculous four-three aggregate victory against Barcelona, the media narrative that "Messi played well, and his teammates should have done more" frustrated me. Any other star player would have been lambasted along with the rest of the team. Messi seems to get special treatment from the football media.

I also appreciate the argument that Messi has never played in any league outside of La Liga, nor for any team other than Barcelona. Would he have been as successful in the Premier League? We'll never know. However, despite my comparatively neutral stance on Messi's ability, I worry that the reader might think I have twisted the following stats in some manner. I can assure you I haven't.

We have studied the standardised nature of finishing ability. Generally speaking, all forwards are just as good at finishing as one another. Even the great Cristiano Ronaldo has underperformed his xG more often than not. Messi is the only player who has consistently outperformed the standards expected of him.

Figure 6-6 shows Lionel Messi's Expected Goals data from the 2014/15 to the 2018/19 campaign. The number of goals which the Argentine scores is breath-taking, but what is more breath-taking is the xG output from which he manages to score them. I cannot state this clearly enough: *no player in current existence manages to consistently outperform his Expected Goals output. Apart from Messi.*

All of Europe's most prolific marksmen, no matter their team or league, generally score the amount you would expect them to score based on the quality of chances presented to them. As we have seen, part of the reason the top strikers amass such large Expected Goals totals is because of their individual skill. Their extra bit of pace, their unique reading of the game, or their skillful dribbling ability allows them to get into high quality positions. Thus, they amass large personal xG totals.

The difference is this: not only does Messi accumulate a lot of xG through his ability to create space for himself and take shots close to goal, but he also *finishes far more chances than would be expected of him*. And he does this consistently. Over the last five seasons, the Argentine has outperformed his xG by 31.18 – he has scored over thirty goals more than expected of him based on the positions from which he shot. Messi is the only player who actually possesses finishing ability which differentiates itself from the norm.

Earlier, I warned against comparing a striker's Expected Goals total to the actual number of goals he has scored. Sadio Mané drastically outperformed his xG in 2018/19 – scoring 22 goals from 16.76(xG). This might prompt us to consider him a clinical finisher. However, the fact that he underperformed his Expected Goals output in several previous seasons indicates that a large component of his remarkable season was chance. Players who incur miraculously prolific seasons will tend to regress to the mean level of performance in the next campaign.

Figure 6-6: Lionel Messi's Expected Goals Performance (2014-2019)

Season	Team	Minutes	Goals	xG	xG Dif	xG90
2018/19	Barcelona	2704	36	26.00	-10.00	0.87
2017/18	Barcelona	2995	34	28.95	-5.05	0.87
2016/17	Barcelona	2832	37	26.89	-10.11	0.85
2015/16	Barcelona	2726	26	27.10	+1.10	0.89
2014/15	Barcelona	3374	43	35.89	-7.11	0.96

Messi is the exception to the rule. By consistently out-performing his Expected Goals output, the Argentine has earned himself the status of being the only reliably clinical finisher in European football.

Lionel Messi's Expected Assists data (*Figure 6-7*) is no less remarkable. In fact, his xA output suggests he would have expected to have clocked even more assists than he has actually mustered. In each of the past three seasons, Messi's teammates have converted fewer goals than the average player would have expected to follow-ing passes made by the Argentine. In total over the past five seasons, Messi could have expected to have made almost ten assists more than he has done in actuality. (This point also serves to further prove the earlier as-sertment that finishing ability is generally standardised. The Barcelona squad is comprised of the best players in the world, yet they actually underperformed expecta-tion in the past three seasons when it came to scoring from Messi's passes).

Figure 6-7 also demonstrates the consistency with which Messi provides for his teammates. The Expected Assists value that a player produces on average per ninety minutes is reflected in their xA90 total. Very few players are able to amass an xA90 total of more than 0.4 over the course of a season. David Silva, wide-ly acknowledged as one of the most creative players in the Premier League, hasn't been able to accumulate more than 0.38(xA90) in any of the last five seasons.

Figure 6-7: Lionel Messi's Expected Assists Performance (2014-2019)

Season	Team	Minutes	Assists	xA	xA Dif	xA90
2018/19	Barcelona	2704	13	15.34	+2.34	0.51
2017/18	Barcelona	2995	12	15.10	+3.10	0.45
2016/17	Barcelona	2832	9	13.96	+4.96	0.44
2015/16	Barcelona	2726	16	15.87	-0.13	0.52
2014/15	Barcelona	3374	18	17.61	-0.39	0.47

The top assisters across all divisions struggle to scratch the 0.40(xA90) mark. In 2018/19, Julien Brandt managed 0.32(xA90), Joshua Kimmich managed 0.40(xA90) and Jaden Sancho managed just 0.30(xA90).

In the last five seasons, Messi hasn't dropped below 0.44(xA90) and averages 0.49(xA90). He has also managed the incredible accomplishment of breaking the 0.50(xA90) boundary twice. Adding Messi's xA90 totals to his xG90 totals means you could expect the Argentine to contribute to around 1.5 goals in every game he plays in, by way of either scoring or assisting.

Our eyes have told us for years that Messi is the best player in the world. The Expected Goals data proves it.

7

BETTING

Can the Expected Goals Method
Make You Rich?

THE EMERGENCE OF EXPECTED GOALS

One collection of people understood the power of Expected Goals long before fans gained wind of the metric. This group knew about xG long before the media adopted it as a form of analysis, and even before professional football clubs realised how useful it could be in the scouting of players. These people were professional gamblers.

In the early pages of this book, I spoke briefly about my introduction to the Expected Goals method. I first came across xG whilst working at a betting consultancy called Smartodds. When I applied for the job, I assumed that my role would be to log stats such as passes, tackles, cards and the like. I was surprised to learn that my role was simply to log the quality of shots.

At first I didn't think too much of it. I came into work each day, watched two to four matches of football, logging the relevant data, before going home again. However, before long I started to think more deeply about what I was doing. Why was I being asked to log the chances which each team were creating? What were the company doing with this data? How did Smartodds turn the raw shot statistics into a turnover of millions of pounds?

After a brief research session, I came across an article on the Expected Goals method. Remember, this was back in 2015. This strand of football analytics was still in its primacy. The only public areas of discussion on the topic of xG were niche online forums. I read about the Expected Goals method, how it worked and what it could be used for. Only then did all the pieces of the puzzle fall into place. Only then did I realise the enormity of what Smartodds were doing, how pioneering their work was, and that I had landed right in the middle of the football data revolution.

Fast-forward half a decade and the Expected Goals method is fairly well-known. Sky Sports and the BBC have made steps towards introducing xG to the masses. A lot of fans have now heard of the phrase "Expected Goals", even if they don't really trust or understand it. However, most people won't know about its early life. They won't know how, back in 2015, Smartodds and other gambling syndicates were using Expected Goals to win hundreds of millions of pounds from the bookmakers.

There is a reason for the lack of knowledge about the early days of xG. Those who understood that the Expected Goals method could be utilised to beat the bookmakers weren't going to give away their secrets to anyone else. Any leak about their system could destroy the edge that they had gained over the competition. Bettors don't want to reveal how they make their money. Thus, the public remained in the dark about Expected Goals for a long time. Only gradually has xG become more mainstream.

WHAT DOES A GAMBLING SYNDICATE LOOK LIKE?

Many readers will not know what a gambling syndicate does, how it is structured or what it really is. This is for the very reason outlined above: professional gamblers try to remain as secretive and enigmatic as possible. They never do interviews with the media, and wish to stay out of the limelight in order to keep their means of analysis secret. Here is all you need to know about Smartodds, an industry-leading gambling syndicate.

Smartodds is a company which collects data on football matches – Expected Goals data, to be specific. Most data companies sell their statistics to the media. We have seen how Opta have become the most prominent football data supplier, selling their stats to companies such as Sky Sports, BBC Sport and *The Guardian* for hefty premiums. In fact, most of the performance stats you see on players and teams will probably have been originally collected by Opta.

Smartodds don't sell their data to the media, but rather to professional gamblers. Their only clients are high-rolling individuals who seek to use the stats to inform their betting. In order to access the company's data, you need to stake a large financial investment in the syndicate.

Opta and Smartodds differ in how they distribute their data. Opta seek as much exposure as possible, so that more media companies will buy their stats off them.

On the other hand, Smartodds are incredibly cautious about sharing their unique models, and only do so to wealthy, trustworthy individuals who are bound by strict confidentiality agreements.

The two companies also differ in the type of data they collect. Opta's data is *descriptive*. They collect and sell stats on possession, passes, tackles and the like. This data offers a pretty good representation of how a team has played, but little in the way of how they will perform in the future. For instance, just because a team has a lot of possession doesn't mean it will win matches – Leicester won the Premier League with the worst passing and possession stats in the division. Opta's primary forms of data is perfect for television broadcasters who look to satisfy consumers with easily digestible stats.

On the other hand, Smartodds' data is *predictive*. They collect stats almost exclusively on Expected Goals, the most profound measure of team and player ability. However, Expected Goals is not immediately palatable to the average football fan – this book is a testament to the lengths one has to go to in order to fully explain xG. This data is useful for gamblers who wish to better predict the outcome of future fixtures. Looking at the Expected Goals scorelines of a team's recent results with give you a good indication of how well they performed, and thus how well they are likely to perform in the future.

Let's look at how Smartodds is structured as a company. There are four different departments, each with their own specific role. The first department are responsible for collecting Expected Goals data – this is the department that I worked for. The second department are responsible for curating and updating the algorithms which the company feeds that data into. The third department are responsible for calculating the bookmakers' odds and deciding which bets to place. The fourth department are responsible for actually placing the bets with the bookmakers, mostly through contacts in Asia.

Let's break each of these subdivisions down further.

Smartodds' first department is known as the "Watchers" group. These employees are not permanently contracted to the company, they are freelancers. This was my role at the company. I was assigned matches to watch, games which varied from the Premier League to the Hungarian second division. I logged Expected Goals data, and was paid £20 for each match that I watched. I would have two monitors on my desk; one screen displaying the game and one screen for the data I was logging into Smartodds' system. Let's say I was watching a match involving Arsenal; I would log every shot that they took against the opposition and every shot that the opposition took against them. So, *the role of the first department is to watch matches and log the Expected Goals data.*

The Expected Goals data collected by the "Watchers" is passed on to Smartodds' second department. This group of employees are quantitative analysts who are tasked with analysing the raw statistics. They feed the stats into the company's complex algorithms, which compute the information and accurately predict match outcomes. For instance, they might feed the Expected Goals scoreline from Arsenal's last six matches into the system, with the aim of determining the likelihood that they will win their next fixture. This branch of the company is filled with the type of computer whizzes you might expect to find working at an investment bank. Smartodds' quantitative analysts (or "quants") are also tasked with constantly developing the algorithms which the Expected Goals data is fed into. These algorithms are obviously kept strictly confidential. So, *the role of the second department is to feed the Expected Goals data into Smartodds' algorithms and work out the probability of match outcomes.*

The third department of the gambling consultancy is responsible for calculating the bookmakers' odds, and comparing them to the probabilities that Smartodds' second department have calculated. For example, suppose that Smartodds' models estimate that (based on the Expected Goals data from their last six matches) Arsenal have a 60% chance of winning their next fixture. This department would look at the bookmakers' odds of this outcome occurring. If they found that the bookmakers were giving Arsenal, let's say, a 50% chance of winning, then they would place a bet on that outcome. In this instance, there is value in the market. The first rule of betting is to find outcomes which the bookies have undervalued. If you think that an outcome has more of a chance of occurring than the bookmakers do, you should place a bet on it. Smartodds' third subdivision will search for any mistakes the bookmakers might have made. So, *the role of the third department is to compare Smartodds' odds to the bookmakers' odds and find value in the market.*

The fourth (and final) department is known as the Bet Placement Team. They are responsible for actually *placing* the bets which the third division have highlighted. The Bet Placement Team use Asian bookmakers to place their wagers, because the markets there are far more liquid than in Europe. The bets which Smartodds place sometimes exceed hundreds of thousands of pounds. Any bet of this magnitude which is placed with one of the European bookmakers would almost certainly be detected, allowing the bookies to adjust their odds to eliminate any loss. In Asia, million pound bets can be placed and go unnoticed by the bookmakers. As such, Smartodds' odds are tailored to the markets in places such as Thailand, Indonesia and China. Using the Asian markets hides the bettors' predictions from the bookmakers, but it can be difficult to access these markets unless you have the right connections. Smartodds' clients are not just paying for the mathematical modelling provided by the company; they are also paying for the black book of contacts which Smartodds has built up in Asia. So, *the role of Smartodds' fourth department is to place the bets recommended by the third department, using the company's Asian contacts.*

The Expected Goals data which Smartodds collect is the foundation upon which their success has been built. There is nothing particularly innovative about the latter three departments. The second department is filled with computer geniuses, but there are many other companies who possess highly skilled individuals capable of curating complex algorithms. The third department is incredibly talented at highlighting where the value in the market is, but this department isn't particularly unique. The fourth department possess the company's black book of contacts which allows them to actually place bets, but there is nothing particularly pioneering in this sector either.

The innovation in Smartodds' approach comes in the *type of data they collect*: Expected Goals data. The work done by the first department, the "Watchers", allows the company to operate in a different league to its competitors. Smartodds were one of the first companies to understand the power of the Expected Goals method, and have been able to make millions as a result.

The Justice Table

Smartodds' analysts operate under a crucial presupposition: *the league table lies.* If the company had a motto, this would be it. It's a fairly counterintuitive concept, and one that many people take issue with. Footballs fans intuitively take the league standings as gospel. The team who is at the top is the best, the team who is at the bottom is the worst, and everyone in between is ranked in order of ability. How can we accept anything else?

The whole power of the Expected Goals method is that it allows us to assess teams based on *performance* rather than *results.* The Expected Goals method ensures that teams who are playing well, but who are being unlucky, get rewarded for their performance. And vice versa, lucky teams are held to account on how well they are actually performing. We have studied how we can measure this in individual matches. If the Expected Goals score of a match finishes *Man City 1.00-1.38 Liverpool,* we can see that it was a tight game that Liverpool probably deserved to win. If Man City actually end up winning the game three-nil with this xG scoreline, we can safely say that they got lucky.

But how can we track the good (or bad) luck of teams over the course of an entire season?

Smartodds' greatest innovation was the development of a "Justice Table": a league table which shows where each team actually *deserves* to be based on the chances they have created and conceded. Teams who are creating lots of high quality chances, dominating matches but not getting the results they deserve, will rank highly in the Justice Table. And vice versa, teams who are performing badly but are luckily picking up a lot of points will rank lowly in the Justice Table. *This makes the Justice Table a more accurate reflection of the ability of teams than the actual league table will.*

In order to generate their Justice Table, Smartodds work out the number of points each team could have expected to take from each match based on the chances that they created and conceded. To do this, they use the mathematical principle of Expected Value. In Chapter 4, we saw how Expected Value can help us work out how much money we can expect to win off a lottery ticket. Expected Value is also the mathematical principle used to work out how many goals a team can expect to score in a match (hence the term "Expected Goals").

Let's now study how Expected Value can help us calculate how many points a team could have expected to take from a match. Expected Points can be a difficult concept to understand at first. The principle of breaking points down into decimals is slightly confusing. How can a team earn, for example, 0.78 points from a match of football? The key thing to remember is that *Expected Points totals reflect the long-term average number of points that a team could have expected to pick up if the game had been played hundreds of thousands of times.*

On 10th March 2019, Arsenal took on Manchester United at the Emirates Stadium in the Premier League. Both teams created a plethora of chances: Arsenal amassed 1.53(xG) whilst Manchester United totaled 2.37(xG). Clearly, the visitors created better chances and deserved to win the match. Despite this, the game finished two-nil to Arsenal. This example perfectly demonstrates how the Expected Goals method can help us separate performance from results. Arsenal didn't perform well, but still managed to get all three points.

Figure 7-1: Expected Goals Map (Arsenal v Manchester United, 10/03/2019)

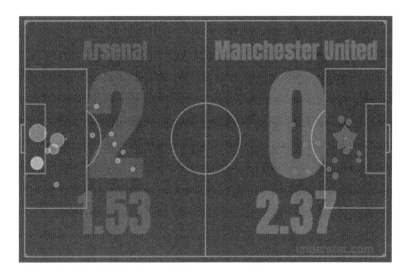

Figure 7-1 outlines the Expected Goals map for the fixture. On the right-hand side of the graphic, the two stars represent Aubameyang's penalty goal worth 0.76(xG) and Xhaka's long-range effort worth 0.02(xG) which found the back of the net. The other small dots represent several low-quality shots taken and missed by Arsenal. On the left-hand side, the collection of larger dots represents the shots taken by Manchester United – a 0.3(xG) effort from Young, 0.43(xG) and 0.48(xG) efforts from Rashford, and a 0.63(xG) attempt from Shaw which hot the post, as well as a plethora of lower value shots. United scored none of these chances.

Clearly, Arsenal were very lucky to win this match. The Expected Goals data tells us that the two-nil scoreline flattered them greatly. In order to quantify this luck, we can work out the number of points that each team could have expected to take from the match based on the chances that they created and conceded. This figure is known as Expected Points (xP).

The maximum number of Expected Points a team can take from a game is three, as this is the maximum points on offer. A team who takes every shot in a match, without conceding a single shot, will amass as much as 3(xP). Vice versa, a team who concedes every shot in a match, without taking one, will collect close to 0(xP). This happens very rarely. Dominant teams normally collect between 2.1(xP) and 2.8(xP), whilst teams who are dominated will earn between 0.1(xP) and 0.5(xP). It is important to note that the Expected Points totals of the two teams do not have to add up to three, as we will see shortly (the fact that draws are worth one point makes the Expected Value equation slightly complex).

Let's break down the process of working out each sides Expected Points total into a series of steps, using the Arsenal-Manchester United match as a guide.

Step One: Find the xG value of each shot which took place in the match and the Expected Goals scoreline. Here are the shot values from the match at the Emirates stadium:

> **Arsenal Shots:** *0.02, 0.02, 0.03, 0.04, 0.04, 0.05, 0.06, 0.07, 0.09, 0.10, 0.12, 0.13, 0.76 = 1.53(xG)*

> **Manchester United Shots:** *0.01, 0.02, 0.02, 0.02, 0.03, 0.05, 0.05, 0.05, 0.06, 0.22, 0.30, 0.43, 0.48, 0.63 = 2.37(xG)*

Step Two: Run a couple of hundred thousand simulations of the match in order to work out the probability of each result occurring. Let's run 100,000 simulations of the Arsenal-Manchester United match, having inputted each team's Shot Probabilities. If this match took place 100,000 times, with the sides creating the exact same quality of chances, how often would each outcome occur? It turns out that Arsenal win roughly 18,690 fixtures, a draw occurs in 22,050 of the matches, and Manchester United win 59,260 matches. Thus, we can state that Arsenal win 18.69% of the time (18,690 out of 100,000), a draw happens 22.05% of the time (22,050 out of 100,000) and Manchester United win 59.26% of the time (59,260 out of 100,000).

Step Three: Once you have the probabilities of each outcome occurring, you can use an Expected Value equation to work out the number of points each team could have expected to take from the match. Let's start with Arsenal. The probability that they pick up all three points is 18.69%, the probability they pick up one point is 22.05% and the probability they pick up no points is 59.26%. The Expected Value equation would look like this:

Expected Points = (Points for Winning x Chance of Winning) + (Points for Drawing x Chance of Drawing) + (Points for Losing x Chance of Losing)

Expected Points = (3 x 0.1869) + (1 x 0.2205) + (0 x 0.5926)

Expected Points = 0.78

Thus, the number of points that Arsenal could have expected to take from this game based on the quality of chances that they created is 0.78. They collect 0.78(xP). We would then carry out the same equation for Manchester United. The Red Devils had a 59.26% chance of victory, a 22.05% chance of drawing and an 18.69% of losing. The equation to work out United's xP is as follows:

Expected Points = (Points for Winning x Chance of Winning) + (Points for Drawing x Chance of Drawing) + (Points for Losing x Chance of Losing)

Expected Points = (3 x 0.5926) + (1 x 0.2205) + (0 x 0.1869)

Expected Points = 2.00

You will recognise this type of formula from Chapter 4, where we studied a handful of examples of how Expected Value equations can help us in various financial settings.

To recap, there are three steps to finding the Expected Points (xP) that a team takes from a match. First, find the value of each of the shots that they took and conceded in the match (the xG data). Second, simulate the match several thousand times in order to work out the probability that each team would win, draw and lose given the shots that they created and conceded. Third, use these probabilities in an Expected Value equation to work out how many points each team could have expected to have earnt.

This all might sound a bit confusing. Don't worry, there are simulators available online which can tell you the Expected Points total of each team when given the shot probabilities from the match. The reader might better understand the process of calculating Expected Points by fiddling about with one of these simulators. My favourite was created by Danny Page and can be found at "https://dannypage.github.io/expected_goals. html". Simply input the xG shot values from a match and the simulator will tell you the percentage chance of each outcome occurring, as well as the Expected Points totals.

When we enter the Shot Probabilities from the Arsenal-Manchester United match into an Expected Points simulator, we find the values are 0.78(xP) and 2.00(xP) respectively. If the match was played hundreds of thousands of times with the same chances falling to either side, Arsenal would pick up an average of 0.73 points per game and Manchester United would gain 2.00 points per game. This reflects the fact that United were the better team. They *deserved* to get more from the game, even if the result actually went against them. If they had been even more dominant, they would have earned even more xP. Conversely, if Arsenal had created more chances, United's xP would have diminished.

———∞∞∞———

If you don't understand the maths, don't worry. You can still understand the principle of Expected Points, even if you don't understand the formula.

Here it is: The Expected Goals scoreline tells you which team performed better. The xG scoreline **Arsenal 1.53-2.37 Manchester United** tells us that the visitors played better than the hosts. They created more chances, and deserved to win the match. Using Expected Value, we can work out that Arsenal deserved to win 0.73 points from the contest, and United deserved to win 2.00 points. These are each team's Expected Points.

Figure 7-2 shows Arsenal's Expected Goals and Expected Points data from their last nine matches of the 2018/19 Premier League season. The first match in the table is the Manchester United game which we have just analysed. As you can see, Arsenal earned 0.73(xP) off the Expected Goals scoreline of **Arsenal 1.53-2.37 Manchester United**. The match finished two-nil to the hosts, despite United's multitude of chances.

Figure 7-2: Arsenal's Expected Goals and Expected Points (2018/19)

Opposition	Score	xG Score	Arsenal xP	Opposition xP
Man United	2-0 (W)	1.53 - 2.37	0.73	2.00
Newcastle	2-0 (W)	1.04 - 0.04	2.36	0.34
Everton	0-1 (L)	0.20 - 2.69	0.08	2.86
Watford	1-0 (W)	2.27 - 1.13	2.24	0.55
Crystal Palace	2-3 (L)	1.54 - 2.56	0.71	2.09
Wolves	1-3 (L)	0.94 - 0.98	1.34	1.33
Leicester	0-3 (L)	0.60 - 3.68	0.08	2.88
Brighton	1-1 (D)	2.36 - 1.91	1.69	1.05
Burnley	3-1 (W)	2.87 - 1.73	2.17	0.64

Hopefully the graphic gives more of an indication of how Expected Points work. The greater the disparity between the Expected Goals totals of the two sides (in other words, the more heavily dominated the match is), the more one-sided the Expected Points totals are weighted.

For instance, look at Arsenal's heavy three-nil defeat at the hands of Leicester. The Expected Goals data justifies the scoreline, as Leicester accumulated a mammoth 3.68(xG) to Arsenal's meek 0.60(xG). In this game, Leicester could expect to take 2.88(xP) from the match, whilst Arsenal only take 0.08(xP).

On the other hand, Arsenal's match against Wolves was a very tight affair. The Gunners accumulated 0.94(xG), whilst Wolves scored a marginally better 0.98(xG). The luck in this game went against Arsenal, who actually lost the game three-one. Despite the defeat, the Gunners' decent performance is still merited with 1.34(xP).

Expected Points totals tell us how many points a team *deserved* to pick up, regardless of the actual result of the match. It allows us to measure *performance*, rather than *results*.

CREATING GOLDEN OPPORTUNITIES

You might have noticed an interesting feature of *Figure 7-2* regarding the match between Arsenal and Wolves. The Expected Goals scoreline for this fixture finished **Arsenal 0.94-0.98 Wolves**, showing that the Gunners created marginally less in terms of scoring opportunities than their opponents. Despite this, Arsenal managed to accumulate 1.34(xP) to Wolves' 1.33(xP). This may seem slightly odd. How can a team who have accumulated a smaller Expected Goals total amass a greater Expected Points total? The answer comes in the fact that *a team who creates a few big chances is more likely to win than a team who creates lots of small chances* (when they accumulate the same (or very similar) xG totals). In order to understand this strange phenomenon, we need to study the mathematical principles of *variance* and *standard deviation*.

Variance tells us to what extent the xG score might have differed. A team who takes more shots than their opponents could potentially score more goals, even if their shots are of a poorer quality and they accumulate a lesser xG total. In our example match, for instance, Wolves took more shots than Arsenal. This meant that, even though the Gunners amassed a very similar Expected Goals total (Arsenal clocked 0.94(xG), Wolves clocked 0.98(xG)), the maximum number of goals they could have scored was lower than Wolves' possible maximum goals total.

Here's an example of the important role that variance plays in xG scorelines. Suppose that we decide to pit two teams against one another; Team Coin versus Team Die. Each time we flip a coin it counts as a 'shot' for Team Coin, whilst each roll of a six-sided die counts as a 'shot' for Team Die. Team Coin's shot 'scores' if it lands on tails but misses when it lands on heads. Team Die's shot 'scores' if a six is rolled but misses if any other number comes up.

In our fabricated match, Team Coin is allowed four shots and Team Die is allowed twelve shots. Seeing that there is a fifty percent chance of a coin landing on tails, and thus scoring a goal, we can assign each of Team Coin's shots 0.5(xG). Team Die has a one in six chance of rolling a six, meaning that each 'shot' has a 16.7% chance of resulting in a goal. Therefore, each of Team Die's attempts can be assigned 0.167(xG).

Team Coin's four shots of 0.5(xG) leaves them with an Expected Goals total of 2, whilst Team Die's twelve 0.167(xG) shots means that they have also amassed a total of 2(xG). The match has played out as following:

Team Coin Shots (xG): 0.5 + 0.5 + 0.5 + 0.5
= 2(xG)

Team Die Shots (xG): 0.167 + 0.167 + 0.167 +
0.167 + (0.167 x 8) = 2(xG)

Essentially what we're saying is that the expected number of occasions that the coin lands on tails when flipped four times is equivalent to the number of occasions that you could expect to land a six if you roll a die twelve times. Both events are expected to occur twice. The Expected Goals scoreline for this match would be two-all.

However, this does not tell the whole story. Although the xG total for each team is equal, the range of goals scored by each team differs significantly. Team Coin can only score a maximum total of four goals, seeing that it has only amassed a total of four shots. In other words, if the coin lands on tails every single time, then Team Coin will have scored four goals. Team Die, on the other hand, has the potential to score twelve goals if a six is rolled on every single occasion. If every single shot worth their 0.167(xG) goes in, then Team Die will have tripled Team Coin's maximum number of goals.

Clearly, the chance that Team Coin flips four tails in a row (6.25%) is far greater than the probability of Team Die rolling twelve sixes in succession (0.02%). However, no matter how small the probability of each occurrence, they both still *could* theoretically happen. The scoreline could range from **Team Coin 0-0 Team Die** to **Team Coin 4-12 Team Die** – and anything in between. The Expected Goals score of **Team Coin 2-2 Team Die** does not represent the room for possible manoeuvre within the scoreline. (Similarly, because Wolves took more shots than Arsenal in their real life fixture, their score-line is exposed to a greater degree of variance). Thus, it is useful to work out the standard deviation associated with the Expected Goals scoreline.

Standard deviation describes how points of data may deviate from the average. A low standard deviation means that the numbers within a pool of data are very close to the average, whilst a high standard deviation would mean they are widely spread out.

Standard deviation is another word for consistency, and is used in a range of fields from accountancy to climatology. In order to explain the formula behind working out standard deviation, let's use the example of a race car driver. Each lap around a circuit is timed. A driver with a low standard deviation of lap times is more consistent than a driver who has a high standard deviation. The more your lap times deviate, the harder it becomes to predict what your next lap time will be. This sounds obvious, right? If a driver clocks the lap time of fifty-six seconds eight times in succession, you can predict with a high degree of confidence that his next lap will be around that same figure. Conversely, a driver whose lap times vary greatly presents a real problem for those trying to forecast his next time. The former driver has a much lower standard deviation than the latter.

The formula for working out the standard deviation for a data group is simple. Suppose that a driver does eight laps around the track, and the time for each individual lap in seconds is as follows: 49, 51, 58, 53, 52, 48, 51, 56. These results are all fairly spread out, and you wish to determine the standard deviation of this data set.

First, you have to find the average lap time, commonly referred to as the *mean* lap time. Add all of the numbers in the data set together and then divide by the number of numbers:

$$(49 + 51 + 58 + 53 + 52 + 48 + 51 + 56) / 8 = \mathbf{52.25}$$

The average lap time for our racing driver is 52.25 seconds, as displayed above. Working out the mean alone is a good indication of what future times the driver is likely to record. However, in order to find the standard deviation, we must work out the difference between each of the points of data and the average. For example, the difference between the first of the driver's lap times (49 seconds) and the average lap time (52.25 seconds) is -3.25 seconds. You then square the difference of each of the individual data points. For instance, -3.25 becomes 10.6. Here is each of these calculations in full:

$$(49 - 52.25)^2 = -3.25^2 = 10.6$$
$$(51 - 52.25)^2 = -1.25^2 = 1.6$$
$$(58 - 52.25)^2 = 5.75^2 = 33.1$$
$$(53 - 52.25)^2 = 0.75^2 = 0.56$$
$$(52 - 52.25)^2 = -0.25^2 = 0.06$$

$$(48 - 52.25)^2 = -4.25^2 = 18.1$$
$$(51 - 52.25)^2 = 1.25^2 = 1.6$$
$$(56 - 52.25)^2 = 3.75^2 = 14.1$$

The final step in the process is to find the average of all of these 'difference' numbers, before taking the square root of that figure:

$$(10.6 + 1.6 + 33.1 + 0.56 + 0.06 + 18.1 + 1.6 + 14.1) / 8 = 9.97$$

$$\sqrt{9}. \ \sqrt{9}. = 3.16$$

Thus, the standard deviation for the driver's lap times is 3.16 seconds. We can now account for the variance in his performance, giving us a more detailed outlining of how the driver's lap times differ. We can compare his standard deviation to that of other drivers, which allows us to work out who is more consistent. A driver whose standard deviation is higher will be more sporadic in his lap times, whilst a driver whose standard deviation is close to zero will be more consistent in his performance.

When calculating the Expected Goals scoreline of a football match, it is worthwhile utilising standard deviation. Some xG totals will be more subject to variance than others (remember that Team Die could have scored anywhere between 0 and 12 goals, whilst Team

Coin could have only scored between 0 and 4 goals. Team Die's Expected Goals total is clearly much more subjected to variance than Team Coin's. Similarly, as Wolves took more shots than Arsenal, their xG total is exposed to greater variance). Accounting for this added variance in the Expected Goals scoreline will add an extra dimension to the analysis. The inclusion of standard deviation in the xG scoreline of our match between Team Coin and Team Die reads like this:

Team Coin 2(xG) (±1) v 2(xG) (±1.29) Team Die

Team Coin's Expected Goals total is subject to a standard deviation of 1, whilst the standard deviation for Team Die's total is 1.29. This reflects that Team Die's xG total is more subjected to variance due to the increased number of shots that they accumulated.

When two teams clock up the same (or a similar) xG total in a match, variance becomes a crucial factor. Our intuition tells us that two teams who score the same number of Expected Goals will win the same number of games in the long run. Surely two teams with the same xG totals must have an equal chance of victory? In reality, it doesn't play out this way.

Let's revert back to our match involving Team Coin and Team Die in order to explain. Having accounted for the standard deviation in the xG scoreline of both Team

Coin and Team Die (±1 and ±1.29 respectively), we can now create a number of simulations of how the match will play out. The analysts who first attempted this were met with a surprising revelation. After conducting thousands of simulations of the match between Team Coin and Team Die, they discovered that Team Coin won 40% of the games, Team Die won 36%, and a draw occurred 24% of the time.

How, when two teams had both amassed exactly 2(xG), could one win more often than the other? Both teams were expected to score two goals given the quality and quantity of shots that they took during the game. Surely they should have an equal chance of winning? Surely Team Die should emerge victorious on just as many occasions as Team Coin (over the long run)?

The results raised an important question: *is it more effective to have a few very good shots than a multitude of poor quality shots?*

The answer to this question could change the way teams approach football. The old cliché goes that if you don't shoot, you won't score. This phrase is regularly used to encourage players to take long-range shots. The theory goes that if you barrage the opposition goal with a host of long shots, one will eventually find its way into the net. Fans and managers alike often urge their team to have more efforts at goal, whilst the media often imply that a team who had fewer shots than their opposition was weaker. The notion that one golden chance should outweigh several speculative efforts at goal could be revolutionary to the way the game is played.

This is what Mark Taylor strove to find out when he analysed a game between Fulham and Manchester United back in 2014. Fulham were outplayed, managing six efforts at goal to Manchester United's thirty-one. Despite this, the match ended in a two-all draw. Taylor noted that despite United's success in accumulating a large quantity of low quality chances, they weren't able to score more goals than the Londoners.

Taylor decided to find out if, when two sides manage to tally up the same xG scoreline, the team who had fewer chances will have the greater probability of winning. In order to test the power of high quality scoring opportunities, Taylor simulated a match between two teams who each amassed a score of 1.2(xG). One team, who we will call "Team Golden Chances" (Team GC), managed only two shots in the match, each one being assigned an xG probability of 0.6. By contrast, the second team, who we shall address as "Team Plentiful Chances" (Team PC), managed twelve efforts at goal, with each one only having a 10% chance of hitting the back of the net. Thus, Team GC (0.6 probability x 2 shots) and Team PC (0.1 probability x 12 shots) both clock a score of 1.2(xG).

Do you recognise this kind of test from somewhere? You should do, because it is essentially the same simulation that we carried out with Team Coin and Team

Die. Both sides are expected to score the same amount of goals, but one has a larger range of scoreline possibilities than the other. Team GC can only score a maximum of two goals, whilst Team PC can score a full twelve if all of their shots go in. The standard deviation of Team Golden Chances is much lower than that of Team Plentiful Chances.

After carrying out twenty-thousand simulations on the match between Team GC and Team PC, Taylor had reached some interesting conclusions. Despite our intuition telling us that the two teams should win the same number of matches, it was in fact Team GC who triumphed more often than Team PC. The team who took two high quality shots won 37.5% of the time, whilst the team who took twelve low quality shots won just 32.1% of the simulated matches which took place. A draw occurred in 30.4% of the games.

This was not a one-off result. Taylor ran several tests with several different xG scorelines and several different shot probabilities for either team. Each and every time, the results showed that the teams who created a few high quality chances won more often than the teams who created a high quantity of low quality scoring opportunities, despite the Expected Goals totals of each team being equal.

He concluded that, when two teams hold the same xG score against one another, it is the team who amassed fewer shots at goal who is more likely to win. Taylor found that as a team produced more and more shots, the range of their likely winning scorelines increased whilst their chance of actually winning diminished. Thus, if you want to increase your goal difference, you are better off taking lots of long-range shots. However, teams can maximise their chance of winning as many points as possible by prioritising the creation of high *quality* chances over the creation of a high *quantity* of chances.

This revelation is thought-provoking. It explains why Arsenal were able to amass 1.34(xP) to Wolves' 1.33(xP), despite accumulating a marginally lower Expected Goals total over the course of the ninety minutes. The Gunners created a few large chances, compared to Wolves' plethora of low quality opportunities.

However, this phenomenon has broader implications. Instead of players being encouraged to try their luck from long range, perhaps teams should attempt to work the ball into the box and create close-range opportunities. Arsenal are the perfect example of a team often criticised for 'over-playing', for passing the ball to death and for not taking enough shots at goal – especially when managed by Arsène Wenger. I once read a stat which asserted that Arsenal had taken the fewest number of shots from outside the box in the Premier League that season. This was meant as a negative statement on Wenger's style of play. In fact, Taylor's studies validate the Frenchman's philosophy of prioritising rare high quality shots over an abundance of low quality attempts.

TURNING DATA INTO CASH

So, how do Smartodds use Expected Points information to develop a Justice Table which ranks every team in the league in order of ability? Well, this is the easy part.

To work out the number of points a team could have expected to have collected over the course of a period of time, you simply have to add up all their Expected Points totals from this period. For example, how many points Arsenal could have expected to have picked up from their last nine fixtures of the 2018/19 season? Adding up all of the Gunners' xP totals from *Figure 7-2* leaves us with 11.40(xP). Thus, Arsenal could have expected to have won 11.4 points from these matches, based on the chances they created and conceded.

In reality, Arsenal picked up thirteen points over the course of these nine matches (four wins, one draw and four losses). An analyst might look at this data and conclude that Arsenal were slightly lucky over this period. The Expected Goals data indicates that they amassed 11.4(xP), when in reality they gained thirteen points. Thus, they overachieved by 1.6 points. You would *expect* them to have scored less points than they did, based on their performances.

It should be obvious how this translates into the Justice Table. Adding up all of a team's Expected Points totals throughout the course of the season will leave you with the number of points that they *deserve to have collected*. In the entirety of the 2018/19 season, Arsenal collected a total of 58.97(xP). This is the number of points which they deserved, when you remove luck from the league table.

In reality, Arsenal accumulated 70 points in 2018/19. This is a much greater than the total you would expect given their performances. In fact, they accumulated 11.03 points more than they deserved. It would be safe to say that The Gunners were extremely lucky to finish as high as they did. In fact, the Premier League Justice Table had them ranked as the seventh best team in the division – with Wolverhampton Wanderers accumulating 59.91(xP) from their matches. *Figure 7-3* shows the top of the 2018/19 Premier League Justice Table.

Figure 7-3: The Top of the Premier League Justice Table (2018/19)

Pos.	Team	Actual Pts	Expected Points	xPts Dif
1	Manchester City	98	90.64	-7.36
2	Liverpool	97	83.45	-13.55
3	Chelsea	72	71.45	-0.55
4	Manchester United	66	61.86	-4.14
5	Tottenham	71	61.44	-9.56
6	Wolves	57	59.91	+2.91
7	Arsenal	70	58.97	-11.03

There are several interesting features to note.

First, notice how the table is ranked according to Expected Points. The Justice Table merits those who have performed well, regardless of whether they have actually picked up points or not. The greater the difference between a team's actual points total and their Expected Points total, the greater impact luck has had on that team.

For instance, Manchester City won the title with 98 points. However, the Justice Table indicates that they were lucky to get that many. Based on the quality of their performances over the season, they should have only reached 90.64. This was still good enough to put them on top of the Justice Table, as Liverpool would have been expected to pick up just 83.45 points. The Reds scored 13.55 points more than their performances merited, making them the luckiest team in the entire division in 2018/19. However, they still finish in 2nd place if the teams are ranked according to performance.

The same cannot be said for Arsenal. Based on the chances they created and conceded, the Gunners should have only scored 58.97 points. This drops them from 5th place in the actual table into 7th place in the Justice Table – moving Manchester United and Wolves above the North London side. The Red Devils would also overtake Tottenham, moving up into fourth place.

The Justice Table might take a while to wrap your head around, but really it makes perfect footballing sense. To recap, the best teams are the ones who create the most chances to score and prevent the opposition from creating opportunities (regardless of whether these chances are scored or not). This is quantified using Expected Goals data. Using xG, we can then work out the probabilities that each team would have won each game. Using this information, we can then assign each team a number of points that they could have expected to gain from each fixture. This Expected Points data can be added up to reveal the *actual* performance levels of teams over the course of a season. Ranking the teams according to their xP will give you a Justice Table.

It should be fairly obvious how Smartodds use this information to win big with the bookmakers. Given that the company have the most accurate gauges of which teams are performing at which level, they can look for errors in the judgement of the bookies.

For example, suppose you were looking to bet on the result of the Europa League final in 2018/19. The final was contested in Baku between Arsenal and Chelsea. You might consult the Premier League table and see that the clubs were only separated by two points at the end of the season. Thus, the two teams must be pretty similar in quality. The final is likely to be a closely contested match, in this case.

However, you might then consult your Justice Table and find that Chelsea accumulated 12.48(xP) more than Arsenal. The Blues actually outperformed the Gunners by a considerable margin, but were less lucky than their London counterparts. On the back of this information, you might notice the undervalued potential of a bet on Chelsea. Indeed, the West London outfit proved their quality with a resounding four-one win over Arsenal.[3]

Smartodds' Justice Table is incredibly sophisticated. The company have founded their success on the ability of this ranking system to better represent the ability of teams than the actual league table does. The Justice Table is based on calculating the Expected Points of each team, which in turn relies on the Expected Goals method. The whole system is founded on the logging of Expected Goals shot values and scorelines. The methodology outlined above has allowed Smartodds to take hundreds of millions of pounds from the bookmakers in the last few years. Whoever said that maths was boring?

---

3 Of course, I have retrospectively used this example to demonstrate how a Justice Table might enable a punter to find value in the market. It is always easy to predict events with the benefit of hindsight.

8

SCOUTING

*What's the Secret Behind Signing
a Hidden Gem?*

FOOTBALL'S "MONEYBALL" STORY

Brentford FC are not a well-known club. The West London outfit have languished in the bottom divisions of English football for the majority of their history. However, in recent years they have gained a reputation as masters of the transfer market. They have consistently been able to identify and sign hidden gems from all corners of Europe. The Bees' recruitment model has allowed them to achieve five consecutive top half finishes in the Championship, despite possessing the fourth lowest wage budget of the twenty-four teams. Brentford's transfer success has allowed them to compete for Premier League football on a shoe-string budget.

As we will soon study in greater depth, Brentford revolutionised their recruitment system after promotion from League One in 2014. Crucially, the club began using mathematical models based on the Expected Goals method to identify undervalued players and bring them into the club. Now, half a decade later, the impact of their new approach is clear to see.

Figure 8-1 displays the most profitable imports that Brentford have made since their 'Moneyball' revolution. (Note that this only includes players who have been bought and then sold on to other clubs. Many other new recruits are still at Brentford. As such, their value is being shown on the pitch rather than in the bank account).

Figure 8-1: Brentford's Most Profitable
Player Recruitments (2014-2019)

Player	Purchased			Sold			Profit
	Year	Club	Fee	Year	Club	Fee	
Neal Maupay	2017	Saint-Etienne	£1.8m	2019	Brighton	£20m	£18.2m
Andre Gray	2014	Luton Town	£500k	2015	Burnley	£12m	£11.5m
Scott Hogan	2014	Rochdale	£750k	2017	Aston Villa	£12m	£11.25m
Chris Mepham	2016	Brentford B	£0	2019	Bournemouth	£11m	£11m
Ezri Konsa	2018	Charlton	£2.5m	2019	Aston Villa	£12m	£9.5m
Ryan Woods	2015	Shrewsbury	£1m	2018	Stoke	£6.5m	£5.5m
Nico Yennaris	2014	Arsenal	£200k	2019	Beijing Guoan	£5m	£4.8m
Jota	2014	Celta Vigo	£1.5m	2017	Birmingham	£6m	£4.5m
James Tarkowski	2014	Oldham	£300k	2016	Burnley	£4.5m	£4.2m
John Egan	2016	Gillingham	£400k	2018	Sheffield United	£4m	£3.6m
Dan Bentley	2016	Southend	£450k	2019	Bristol City	£4m	£3.55m
Romaine Sawyers	2016	Walsall	£300k	2019	West Brom	£2.9m	£2.6m
Moses Odubajo	2014	Leyton Orient	£1m	2015	Hull	£3.5m	£2.5m
Maxim Colin	2015	Anderlecht	£900k	2017	Birmingham	£3m	£2.1m
Florian Jozefzoon	2017	Jong PSV	£900k	2018	Derby County	£2.8m	£1.9m
Total			£12.5m			£109.2m	£96.7m

Figure 8-1 demonstrates the limited resources with which Brentford can operate. Before the 2019 Summer transfer window, the largest fee that the club had ever forked out on a player was £3.5m for Algerian winger Said Benrahma. In their 129-year history up to the Summer of 2019, Brentford had spent less than £25m on player recruitment. Even since their promotion to the Championship, they have only possessed a modest transfer budget. However, what they have achieved with their shoe-string finances is exceptional.

The players in *Figure 8-1* were brought to the club for £12.5m, a measly sum for a modern day football club. However, Brentford have managed to sell these players on for a total of £109.2m, leaving them with a staggering profit of £96.7m. To put that into perspective, *Brentford didn't spent more than £2.5m on a single one of these players, yet were able to turn over £96.7m profit.*

The key to Brentford's transfer market success is their ability to identify undervalued talent. Many of their signings come from the lower leagues of English football or from obscure European divisions. Brentford's most profitable signing, Andre Gray, was recruited from fifth tier Luton Town. Meanwhile, Scott Hogan was plucked from a fourth tier Rochdale team. The Bees are consistently able to recognise players who are unrecognised by the rest of world football. Brentford's mathematical approach to identifying talent has enabled them to sign high quality players for rock bottom prices.

Brentford's 'Moneyball' approach is centred around the Expected Goals method. In the same way that Smartodds use the metric to identify undervalued bets, Brentford use xG to identify undervalued players. In fact, Smartodds and Brentford are both owned by the same man, the most mysterious football revolutionary of modern times.

Smartodds was founded in 2004 by Matthew Benham, a professional gambler who had made millions through correctly predicting the outcome of football matches. Benham is an enigmatic character. He prefers to stay out of the limelight as much as possible, so much so that it is almost impossible to find a single interview with him anywhere. What we do know is that Benham is one of the most successful professional gamblers in recent history.

The Englishman studied at the University of Oxford between 1986 and 1989, where he obtained his Bachelor of Arts degree in Physics. After graduating, he secured his first job as an associate at Yamaichi International Europe in 1990. He left the company after a year, moving to General RE Financial Productions. In the late 1990's, he became Vice President of the Bank of America. Benham had slowly worked his way up the career ladder, but his life was about to take a dramatic change of direction.

Benham transitioned into the gambling sector when he became a trader for Premier Bet in 2001. He began to apply his knowledge of financial markets to the field of sports betting. After leaving Premier Bet, he turned to professional gambling. His analytical mind allowed him to turn over hundreds of thousands of pounds through betting on football fixtures. Benham was making it on his own, but soon he saw the need to scale up his betting project.

In 2004, Benham set up his own gambling consultancy, Smartodds. We have already studied how Benham structured the company. Smartodds collects and sells data to high-rolling professional gamblers. These wealthy punters pay hefty sums in order to utilise Smartodds' state-of-the-art analytical models. Benham himself also makes use of the company's services in order to aid his own betting. Smartodds realised the power of the Expected Goals method before anyone else and were able to make millions as a result. As the company became increasingly profitable, so too did their owner. Before long, Benham had become a self-made multi-millionaire.

In 2005, Benham's boyhood football club ran into serious financial trouble. Brentford FC, a small West London club who have achieved little success since World War Two, were on the brink of administration.

Benham anonymously invested £500,000, saving the club from going under. The only details made public at the time was that the mystery investor was an earnest fan who wanted to rescue the club.

Benham worked closely with Brentford until June 2012, when he bought out enough shares to become majority owner of the club. At this point, the team were fighting for promotion from League One. Benham began using Smartodds' data to highlight players who the Bees might be able to recruit for modest sums. However, Brentford's financial insecurity meant that transfers could not exceed tens of thousands of pounds. Benham did not have the resources to compete in the transfer market.

This changed in 2014 when Brentford got their big break. After just two years with the professional gambler as their owner, Benham's team were promoted to the Championship. The club had not competed at this level for twenty-two years. The 2014/15 season would see them lock horns with the likes of Leeds, Fulham and Watford in the second tier of English football. Their new status as a second division side meant that Benham finally had the capital to start manipulating the transfer market.

However, operating within the Championship presented Benham with a new host of problems. How does a club who can only afford a yearly wage bill of £14.7m compete in a league where the average annual wage expenditure is £39m? How does a club who can only pull in attendances of 11,000 fans compete with clubs who can bring in five times that number? How does a club who cannot afford to make signings of more than a couple of million pounds compete with teams who are spending in excess of £40m every Summer? Essentially, how does David compete in an entire league filled with Goliaths? These are the questions which faced Matthew Benham's Brentford when they arrived in the Championship.

Figure 8-2: Championship Annual Wage
Expenditure (£millions) (2018/19)

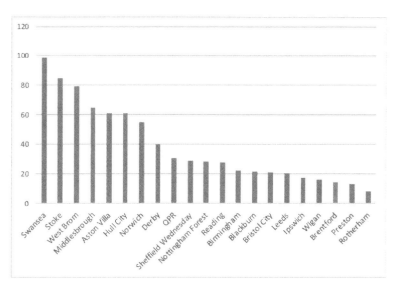

Figure 8-2 demonstrates the full extent of Brentford's problem. Whilst the average annual wage expenditure of a Championship club in 2018/19 was over £39m, Brentford spent just £14.7m. The Bees were one of only three teams to possess a wage budget of less than £15m. In a sport where finances are so directly correlated with success, Matthew Benham's club would be expected to be consistently fighting relegation.

Brentford are a small club. They have a small stadium, which only holds 12,000 fans (*Figure 8-3*). They have a small fanbase, boasting only just over one-hundred thousand followers on Twitter (*Figure 8-4*). Despite playing in the second division of English football, their facilities and their finances could be more accurately compared to a third or fourth division team. They are regularly taunted with cries of 'tin-pot' from the fans of much larger opposition.

Benham realised that Brentford did not have the resources to compete in the Championship. Even with his backing, the club were always going to be outspent by almost every other team in the league. However, Benham's ownership of Brentford gave them an edge. The club couldn't outspend their opponents, but they could *outthink* them. Equipped with Smartodds' data, Benham could use advanced statistical modelling to make more intelligent signings and manipulate the transfer market to their favour.

Figure 8-3: Championship Club Stadium Size (2018/19)

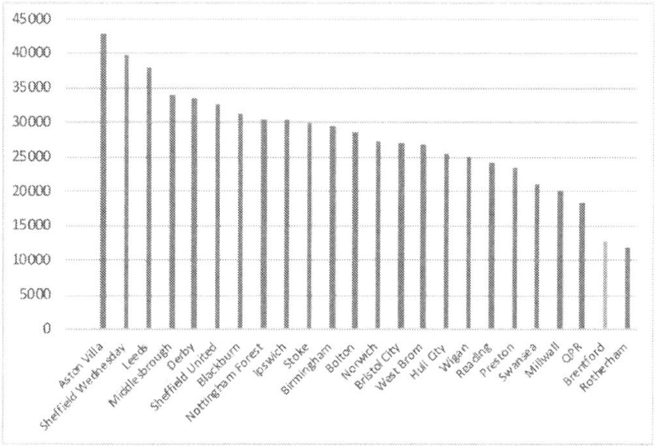

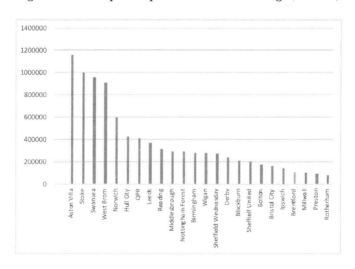

Figure 8-4: Championship Club Twitter Followings (2018/19)

However, this is more easily said than done. For one thing, revolutionising the whole philosophy of a football club away from an old-school line of thought and towards a philosophy based on mathematical modelling is not an easy task. Benham planned to disregard conventional scouting methods, placing a greater emphasis on Smartodds' data and his own analytical tools. The owner was taking a big risk. We have already seen how traditionalists can react to the rise of analytics within football. Benham was putting himself in jeopardy of being ostracised by fans and the media if his radical methods were to fail.

However, Benham's whole career had been built around taking calculated risks. First as a trader, then as a professional gambler, the Brentford owner had earned millions through betting. His system hadn't failed him before, but could it really bring success in the football transfer market?

THE FOOTBALL STOCK MARKET

Brentford's approach to buying and selling players is similar to a trader's approach to the stock market. Each football player represents an intrinsic value; a sum of money that he is worth to the club. In football, the wealthiest clubs are generally the most successful. The correlation between the depths of the owner's pockets and the loftiness of his club in the league table is overwhelmingly strong. Thus, Benham's simple aim is to build a squad which is as valuable as possible, whilst at the same time spending as little money as possible.

Brentford are a poor club. They have been languishing in the third and fourth tiers of English football for most of their existence. However, since Benham took over, the club have been enjoying their most successful period for decades. The key to Benham's success has been his ruthless approach to buying and selling players. Smartodds' data allows him to identify undervalued prospects. The trick to mastering the transfer market is to find the unappreciated players, the hidden gems which can add more to your team than their price tag suggests. Benham has developed a system which highlights such players, allowing him to build a squad far more valuable than the money it cost to buy.

However, importing players is only half the story. It is obvious that you want to buy the best commodities for the cheapest prices. In our everyday lives we live by this principle. When all other things are equal, we will always plump for the inexpensive options. What makes Benham's approach so shrewd is his approach to *selling* players.

Most football supporters are desperate to see their club retain their best talents. The fan favourites who grace the turf every week are loved and cherished by those in the stands. However, Brentford's philosophy is to be just as eager to sell your best players as to buy new ones. This may seem counterintuitive, but the Bees are always aware which of their players might be overvalued by other clubs. Benham would be happy to sell a player who other sides are willing to pay in excess of his *actual* value for, regardless of the footballer's reputation amongst the fans. That money can then be reinvested into finding more undervalued prospects.

There are plenty of inefficiencies within the transfer market. Certain biases can lead to players becoming criminally overrated. Indeed, most scouts are profoundly insufficient at accurately determining the value of footballers. Benham and his analysts are always looking to exploit this. They consistently look out for clubs who might be willing to pay more for a player than he is worth.

Brentford's philosophy is perfectly demonstrated in the club's buying and selling of striker Andre Gray. In 2014, Benham's statistical models highlighted the striker when he was playing in the Conference for Luton Town. Gray was in fine scoring form, but few clubs in the higher divisions were willing to take a chance on a player from the fifth tier of English football. Nevertheless, Benham's models projected that Gray was performing at the level of a decent Championship forward. Benham saw the undervalued potential of Gray and Brentford snapped him up for a measly £500k.

Gray's transfer was met with a fair amount of scepticism from Bees fans. The striker had never played professional football before in his career, having only ever performed in non-league. Despite this, Gray took to the Championship with ease. The striker scored eighteen goals in his first season at Brentford, helping the team reach fifth place in the league. Andre Gray quickly became a fan favourite.

Benham's system had succeeded in identifying an extremely talented player who was undervalued by the rest of the footballing world. However, the story doesn't end there. Gray's whirlwind first season had seen him draw attention from several other clubs. Benham realised that Gray had become greatly overvalued in the eyes of potential suitors. Brentford knew that players who have an exceptional season often regress to the mean. Benham anticipated that Gray would not do as well the following season if he remained at Brentford. The striker's stock was nearing its peak, Benham concluded. In the transfer market, as in all markets, the right time to sell is when the price of an item is as inflated as it will get.

Benham decided to enter talks with other clubs over the signing of Andre Gray. A few weeks later Gray was transferred to Burnley for a fee which eventually rose to a whopping £12m, comfortably the largest sum that Brentford had ever received for a single player. The West London club had bought a player for £500k and sold him for £12m just one season later. Benham had traded

Gray for twenty-four times as much as he had acquired him for.

Benham's philosophy is centred around using innovative recruitment techniques to find undervalued players. Whether that be bringing in a free transfer whose signing carries little risk, or spending a little more cash on a prospect who could become a top level footballer, the key is to spot the players who add more value to the squad than they will cost you to bring them in. Conversely, by selling players who other clubs are willing to pay over the odds for, Benham makes sure that his squad becomes increasingly valuable. In a sport where the wealthiest teams have a far greater chance of succeeding, Benham has mastered the art of steadily increasing the affluence of Brentford.

Billy Beane highlighted the need to be constantly "upgrading" the quality of his playing staff. This is exactly what Matthew Benham has done. He invests money on players, seeking a large return on those investments, then looking to reinvest the money he has made on even better players. Invest, cash in, reinvest, repeat.

Despite Benham's transfer market philosophy working wonders at Brentford, fans often misunderstand the logic behind it. When Andre Gray was sold to Burnley, for example, Brentford supporters didn't see it as a shrewd piece of business. The supporters simply saw a Gray-shaped hole in their starting line-up. They didn't understand why Benham had sold one of their best players to a rival in the same division. The selling of a fan-favourite does seem to defy intuition, even if it makes economic sense. Football fans must try to accept that their club will sell its best players. In fact, fans should *encourage* and *want* their club to do so. Similarly, owners and managers should learn to spot signs of decay in their squads, and cash in before their players' value deteriorates.

Benham doesn't view each player as a player, but as an amount of money. Each player represents an intrinsic value of worth, like stocks in the stock market. A team is essentially a portfolio of financial assets. When signing a player, Benham always considers their re-sale value. Younger players are clearly much more profitable than older ones. They can be developed and sold for a much greater sum than they were bought for. It is little coincidence that Brentford boasted either the youngest or the second-youngest squad in each of the 2016/17, 2017/18 and 2018/19 seasons. In fact, at the start of the 2018/19 campaign, Brentford's squad didn't include a single player over the age of thirty.

When a club is willing to pay more money for your player than he is actually worth, you should sell him. When you spot a player who you could buy for less than he is worth, you should buy him. These are simple principles of investment, yet they are criminally neglected in the world of football.

Why is football so ignorant in this regard? For one, owners, managers and fans alike are blinded my emotion. Football is an incredibly sentimental game, and it is hard to keep an unbiased view of what is going on around you. Fans become emotionally attached to players, and when they leave it can be hard to let them go. Managers must separate themselves from such sentiments and act in a rational manner to ensure the best possible future for their club.

Brentford have actually branded themselves as a "selling club" to potential signings. Benham and his team, when attempting to lure a player to Griffin Park, will point to the several players that Brentford have sold to Premier League clubs as examples of where their potential recruit could end up. Brentford brand themselves as a stepping stone to top flight football. 'If you come and play well for us', Benham will say, 'then we will happily sell you to a Premier League team'.

This philosophy was unravelled publicly after goalkeeper Daniel Bentley signed for Brentford in the Summer of 2016. Bentley openly admitted that he saw Brentford as a stepping stone to Premier League football. Fans were left bemused by the idea that a newly-signed player was already talking about leaving for a bigger club. However, this is the philosophy which Brentford are happy to promote. The Bees sign undervalued players when they are cheap and young, they develop them, and then they sell them to bigger teams when they become overvalued.

Now let's turn our attention away from Brentford's general philosophy, and towards how the Bees actually identify hidden gems. How has Smartodds helped Brentford become one of Europe's most overachieving clubs? And how does Matthew Benham use data to recruit undervalued talents?

THE CLUB STRUCTURE OF THE FUTURE

In 2014, after Brentford were promoted to the Championship, Matthew Benham's was to overhaul the structure of the club. Benham reorganised the backroom staff, taking power out of the hands of the manager and placing into the hands of data analysts and two Directors of Football. This innovation has made the West London outfit more efficient, more resourceful and more professional in their approach to decision-making. Studying the 'European' structure of Brentford is crucial if we are to understand how they have utilised the Expected Goals method to achieve success.

We begin our behind-the-scenes tour of Brentford's set-up by meeting the various protagonists responsible for maintaining the club's model. There are three tiers to the club's backroom staff. At the top of the pyramid is the owner, Matthew Benham. Beneath him are two

Directors of Football who, at the time of writing, are Phil Giles and Rasmus Ankersen. Finally, there exists the Head Coach and the rest of the coaching staff. At the time of writing, Thomas Frank is the Head Coach of Brentford. The club's three tiers of management (the owner, Directors of Football, and Head Coach) make up what will be referred to as the 'management team'. Brentford's structure is different to any other club in the country.

The roles of the owner, the Directors of Football and the Head Coach can be likened to the hands of a clock, each responsible for a certain aspect of the club's time-keeping needs. The Head Coach is responsible for the second's hand of the clock (day-to-day strategy). The Directors of Football, Ankersen and Giles, are responsible for the minute's hand (medium-term strategy, focused on transfers and player replacement). The board, particularly Benham, are responsible for the hour's hand (long-term strategy and objectives).

Let's start at the top of the pyramid. Matthew Benham is the owner of Brentford; the man merited with founding and leading Brentford's 'Moneyball' approach. He could be considered football's answer to Billy Beane. However, Benham is extremely reluctant to engage with the media. Unlike most multi-millionaires, Benham prefers to stay as far from the limelight as possible. The sustainability of Benham's ground-breaking methods is dependent on his ability to slip under the radar. As such, the owner of Brentford cuts a very mysterious and elusive figure.

Benham's role within the Brentford structure is that of a typical owner. He runs the club, chooses which staff to hire or sack and is responsible for generally overseeing the long-term future of Brentford FC. He has long since realised the unsustainable running costs of Griffin Park, the Bees' home ground since 1904. As such, the owner is building a new stadium for the club less than a mile from their current home. The new stadium will hold around 18,000 fans, rather than the 12,000 at Griffin Park, and will cost a lot less to upkeep. As aforementioned, Benham's role can be likened to that of the hour hand – he keeps an eye on the long-term future of the club.

When restructuring Brentford, Benham decided to employ two Directors of Football. The Director of Football role is fairly uncommon in English football, but has been used to great success in Europe. Essentially, the Directors of Football act as the minute hand in Brentford's clockwork structure. They keep tabs on when each of the players' contracts are running out and try to plan at least two seasons ahead when it comes to player arrivals and departures. For example, if a player who has one year left on his contract looks like he won't sign a new one, the Directors of Football might decide to sell him whilst they can still cash in on him. Similarly, the Directors of Football track the club's long-term transfer targets, keeping an eye on the contracts of potential recruits.

At Brentford, the manager has little say over player recruitment – this job is left to the Directors of Football. Upon appointing Phil Giles and Rasmus Ankersen as Co-Directors of Football in 2015, Benham stated that 'the role is a big one and splitting it means we can add the expertise of both of them to our management structure'.

Phil Giles had previously worked as the Head of Quantitative Sports Research at Smartodds since 2011. Benham stated that Giles 'is someone who has excellent football knowledge and the analytical skills to assess players, tactics and teams in the way we want to'. Every decision made by the Directors of Football is made with the support of profound statistical analysis. It is no wonder that a man who has a PhD in Statistics is at the forefront of Brentford's model.

Thomas Frank, the Brentford manager, currently represents the final hand of the Brentford's clock structure; the second's hand. Matthew Benham deals with long-term projects (such as the building of the new stadium), Phil Giles and Rasmus Ankersen deal with the medium-term projects (player recruitment and contract negotiations) and the Brentford manager deals with the short-term problems (managing the playing staff and developing tactics for upcoming matches).

Being the manager of Brentford under Benham's 'Moneyball' system differs considerably from being the manager of any other team in England. Whilst managers usually have power over every major decision that a club makes, Brentford's manager has been stripped of most of the traditional duties. As aforementioned, Benham's Directors of Football are in charge of player recruitment. They, alongside a team of analysts, use data to unearth undervalued prospects and bring them to Brentford. Thus, the role of Thomas Frank is simply to manage the playing staff that he is given.

When Benham decided to take the power of veto out of the manager's hands in 2015, it caused quite a stir. At the time Brentford was managed by the popular Mark Warburton, the man who had led the club to promotion from League One. Warburton and Benham locked horns over how the club should be structured. Warburton was a traditionalist. He rejected Benham's proposal to use the Expected Goals method to drive player recruitment. Warburton also disliked the idea that the power of making signings would be taken out of his hands. He refused to work under the 'Moneyball' philosophy that Benham envisioned for the club. The conflict ended in the departure of Warburton, much to the dismay of the fans. Benham and the newly-appointed Giles and Ankersen were criticised by large sections of the Brentford fanbase. The media branded Brentford as a 'circus', branded Benham as a tyrannical owner and branded Brentford's statistical methods as idiotic. Few believed that the analytical models which had achieved success in baseball could be translated to a sport as fluid and dynamic as football.

Since then, Benham's reinventing of Brentford's structure has been validated. Benham's restructuring of the club took power out of the hands of the manager and put them into the hands of unemotional statistical analysts who could make better decisions. This laid the foundations for their transfer market success. Modern day Head Coaches operate in dictatorial systems, where they have complete power to sign whoever they want and play in whatever style they want. This creates several problems.

Firstly, managers change clubs extremely frequently. A manager who is underperforming is likely to be sacked. Similarly, a manager who is overperforming is likely to be poached by a bigger club. Very few managers stay at a club for more than a handful of seasons. Indeed, the average lifetime of a manager is now under a year.

The changing of managers often comes at a huge cost to clubs. In the first instance, a club who sacks its manager will have to buy out his contract for a hefty fee. But even if the manager chooses to leave, or is poached by a bigger club, it is expensive for the club. New managers will look to implement their own style of play and bring in new players who fit into that style. Newly hired managers often carry out a radical overhauling of the club's playing staff. They look to spend money on players who fit their tactical model. Thus, a club who regularly changes managers also ends up spending a lot of money on new players, and discarding the old ones who won't work under the new system. This is a wildly inefficient way of operating.

Matthew Benham has created a remedy for such inefficiency. An additional role of the Directors of Football at Brentford is to ensure that the brand of football played by the club remains the same from the youth team up to the first team. Thus, the style of football adopted by the club is continuous, regardless of new managers who might come and go in quick succession. This may seem a small measure, but it allows the club to run much more efficiently when their managers are poached by larger clubs.

The second reason Benham decided to take power out of the hands of the manager was to utilise the wisdom of the collective. A manager is likely to have wide gaps in his footballing knowledge, leading to poor decision-making abilities. Brentford's manager is aided by two Directors of Football, a team of analysts and even the owner himself, who all take part in the major decision-making processes. Every time Brentford decide whether or not to sign a player, or negotiate a new contract with one, it has to be approved by a committee consisting of the manager, the Directors of Football, analysts and the owner. The manager, as a member of the committee, does have some say over each new signing that the club makes. Brentford would rarely sign a player whom the Head Coach doesn't like. However, the manager cannot sign a player without first consulting the committee. If the player ranks poorly in Benham's statistical models, there is very little chance of the club signing him. This 'cabinet' style of working is similar to how the senior members of the British parliament convene to discuss matters of the state. Benham's managers operate within a democracy, not a dictatorship.

The idea behind this model is that personal biases are quashed by the decision of the collective. In traditional recruitment setups, a manager is free to sign any player he likes. Conversely, he can easily disregard any player whom he doesn't like. This means that his own personal biases and beliefs may hold him back. For example, if a manager believes that small players hold little value because they are weak, there will be no one there to correct his mistake[4]. His team will suffer because of a personal prejudice that he holds. The use of a transfer committee combats this by eliminating individual biases. One manager will have a lot of wrongly informed beliefs. By having several people all contribute

---

4 Such a belief used to be common in football. Scouts were told to look for strong, physical athletes. In reality, small players' low centre of gravity gives them an advantage, with agility now being recognised as a particularly dangerous attacking weapon.

their ideas and opinions, you are increasing the sample size of knowledge that you can use. The individual flaws of each person are cancelled out by the shared experience of the collective.

The final reason for Benham's decision to take decision-making power out of the hands of Brentford's manager and place it into the hands of two Co-Directors of Football is to allow for rational, data-driven decisions to be made over irrational, emotional ones. Football is an incredibly emotive sport and managers tend to be especially impassioned individuals. The second chapter of this book explored the tension between the traditionalists and the revolutionaries. The former favour 'gut-feeling' when it comes to decision-making, whilst the latter choose to utilise data and analytics. Brentford's 'Moneyball' model has been founded on a greater emphasis on statistical analysis. Using mathematical models based on the Expected Goals method can more profoundly reveal the ability of teams and players than the human eye can. It was Billy Beane who stated that "those who get kicked out of casinos are the card counters, not the gamblers basing decisions on gut-feeling".

Brentford have led the mathematical revolution in football. Even during matches, their manager is equipped with a team of analysts who give him advice through an ear-piece. These analysts usually sit with half a dozen laptops adjacent to the media section inside the stadium. Their job is to recommend which substitutions the manager should make, as well as when to make them, based on key performance indicators that are being logged and scrutinised during the game. As a result, even decisions on the in-match substitutions are data-driven, rather than being based on gut-feeling. The analysts are able to separate themselves from the emotion of the game, something that a manager often struggles to do. Head Coaches are too involved to make clear and concise judgements. When making substitutions, they may let the extremities of their emotions take the better of them. Whether it be fury at a refereeing decision or euphoria at a goal being scored, a coach's emotions can blind him from making rational decisions. The analysts can offer objective advice, supported by data, suggesting what tactical decisions will give the team the best chance of victory.

Other English clubs have started to follow Brentford's suit in recent years, Liverpool being the most notable example. The Reds hired Michael Edwards as Sporting Director and have begun using mathematical modelling in their recruitment. Liverpool's fortunes have improved drastically since these innovations. However, the outstanding majority of football clubs still maintain a structure that has remained unchanged for decades. These systems are relics of a less technologically advanced era. The future will almost inevitably see the rise of more democratic systems, and the hiring of more analytical teams to steal decision-making influence from managers.

Most managers might be unhappy with power being taken out of their hands, as was the case with Mark Warburton when Matthew Benham introduced his model to Brentford. However, there is a positive aspect to this change for Head Coaches. In existing structures, the great power of the manager makes them an easy scapegoat. They come under a great amount of criticism when their team isn't performing well. A poor run of form will often result in the manager losing his job. A shift to a more collective and democratic system, such as the one at Brentford, will make the role of the manager more stable. It will become harder to sack the man in charge, leading to a greater job security for managers. This stability can surely only be a good thing for both managers and the football clubs that they run.

A Global Justice Table

The world of football tends to view the league table as the all-important factor in deciding which teams are the best. The team who wins the title is considered the best team and the team who finishes bottom are considered the worst team – it would be illogical to suggest anything otherwise. League tables are taken as gospel.

In actuality, the league table offers an inaccurate depiction of each team's ability. Thirty-eight games (or forty-six for the Football League fans amongst us) is still a small sample size of data. The fact that so many teams are separated by just a handful of points at the end of a season is a testament to this. Manchester City fans will testify that entire campaigns can be decided with the final kick of the ball. When each individual game is governed by so much luck, and each season often comes down to an individual game, it follows that the fortune of many clubs comes down to utter randomness.

This may be hard for some to hear. We would like to believe that success is determined purely by factors such as skill and work-rate. It can be difficult to accept that a whole season can sometimes come down to utter chance. It seems unfair that luck can play such a large role in football, and this is probably why we tend to undervalue the impact that it has on the game. We would prefer to believe that football is deterministic; that managers and players have complete control of whether they win or lose. Rasmus Ankersen, Co-Director of Football at Brentford, stated that "telling people the league table lies is like telling people that the Earth is flat. All their preconceptions are being challenged, and the media won't accept it". In reality, randomness heavily influences the league table standings.

This is good news for those who are able to quantify the uncertainty of the beautiful game. Matthew Benham has stated that he will never judge his managers based on where they stand in the league table, he will judge them based on their *performances*. The difference being that, whilst the league standing of a team will fluctuate due to luck, the performance of a side is completely within the manager's control. Benham bases his whole philosophy on this vital definition. All a manager can do is ensure his team puts in decent performances. If they are unlucky, losing when they perform well, an owner should not lambast his manager. Performance is deterministic, league ranking is not.

By monitoring the Expected Goals results of every club in Europe (through Smartodds), Benham is able work out which teams are *performing* at the highest standard. This xG data strips luck and randomness from football. As well as seeing how many goals each team is scoring, Benham's analysts can monitor how many goals a team *deserves* to be scoring based on their performances. I cannot emphasise enough how important this point is to grasp.

Every league which Smartodds collects data on can be translated into a Justice Table. These Justice Tables will incorporate Expected Points instead of actual points and Expected Goals instead of actual goals. One can even calculate the Expected Goal difference of each team; simply take the total xG that a team has scored and subtract the total xG they have conceded. We have already studied how Smartodds have used Justice Tables to succeed in the world of gambling. The company are able to identify which teams have been lucky and which have been unlucky. Thus, they have a more accurate gauge of team performance than the bookmakers.

However, the innovation goes even further. From looking at past matches between sides from different divisions, Smartodds' analysts have the ability to create a *Global Justice Table*; one giant league table which incorporates every professional football team that Smartodds collects data on.

The Global Justice Table is formed by analysing matches between teams from through different leagues, allowing Smartodds' analysts to accurately gauge the difference in performance levels between divisions. Each season, hundreds of matches take place between sides from different leagues. Within England, these matches take place in competitions such as the FA Cup, the League Cup and the EFL Trophy. Almost every team in England is eligible to take part in the FA Cup, a tournament which often pits lower league sides against the giants of the Premier League. The League Cup includes teams from the top four divisions of English football. The EFL Trophy is contested between teams who reside in the third and fourth tiers of the English pyramid. Most of the games in these competitions feature teams from different divisions playing one another. By collecting the Expected Goals data from matches between teams of different divisions, Smartodds' analysts are able to accurately gauge the difference in playing ability between leagues.

For example, let's say that Smartodds have collected data on hundreds of matches in which one team is from the Premier League and one is from the Championship. The analysts can create algorithms and formulae to determine the extent to which the Premier League sides tend to dominate the game. Do they create far more scoring opportunities than the teams from the division below, or do the Championship clubs tend to hold their own? From analysing the stats, they can formulate a concise image of the gap in standard between the two divisions. The same process can easily be repeated with matches between teams from the Championship and League One, from League One and League Two, and so on and so forth.

In fact, every league in Europe is comparable to one another, as long as matches frequently occur between sides from the different divisions. The Champions League and Europa League competitions facilitate matches between clubs of different countries throughout the continent. Additionally, multiple friendlies are played between teams from different European leagues. Thus, any league in Europe can be compared to any other league in which teams from the two countries compete. Smartodds analysts can take data from matches between, for example, Premier League and La Liga clubs and see who tends to perform better. They can utilise their advanced models to see which league generally operates at a higher level.

However, one cannot simply state that one league is better than another. A team who is at the bottom of one division will almost certainly be worse than a team who is at the top of another. Although one could argue that the Premier League is of a higher quality than Ligue 1, very few would argue that Bournemouth are a better side than Paris Saint-Germain. European football is like an enormous spider web. Each match which takes place between two clubs of different divisions is the equivalent of a single thread. By plugging the information from each individual thread into their models, the analysts at Smartodds can create an accurate assessment of each team's ability based on their ranking in their own "domestic" Justice Table, coupled with the ranking of their division amongst Europe's other divisions.

At the end of this data analysis, the Smartodds analysts can compile a Global Justice Table that incorporates every team that they collect data on. Every single team in Europe is lumped into one giant league table, each ranked alongside one another as if in one huge division. Whenever your club plays a match, you naturally consider the implications on your league standing. "If we win, and that other team lose, we could move up to seventh place", the anonymous fan might state. However, within Matthew Benham's framework, each club is not just competing with teams in its actual division (be it

Premier League, Championship, Algerian Second Division, whatever), it is also competing with *every other professional football team in Europe.* A fan with access to Benham's global league table could support Oldham Athletic and excitedly exclaim, "If we win today, and Ordabasy of the Kazakhstan Premier League lose, we could move up to 675th in the Global Justice Table!"

Actually this is not what the fan would be saying at all. Wins, draws and losses do not count for anything in Benham's system. What counts is the Expected Goals scoreline from each match. The fan would be more correct in exclaiming that, "If we create a large number of high quality chances, whilst simultaneously conceding very few, we will amass a dominant Expected Goals scoreline and thus win a large number of Expected Points. This means that we will move higher up in both our domestic Justice Table and the Global Justice Table!"

Benham's system gives analysts an idea of which teams are performing at the highest level when luck is stripped from the equation. For coaches, scouts and gamblers, performance is all that should matter. The rest is down to randomness. You may not be able to win titles by amassing favourable Expected Goals scorelines, by accumulating a large number of Expected Points or by finishing first in the Justice Table, but you certainly give yourself the best chance of doing so.

UNEARTHING HIDDEN GEMS

The data that Smartodds collects has two primary functions; to inform the professional gamblers who buy the stats from the company and to assist Brentford in their recruitment of players. In Chapter 7, we saw how Smartodds' Justice Tables aid the professional gamblers who purchase such data. The company's clients simply have to cross-reference Smartodds' Justice Tables with the *actual* league tables. This reveals which teams have actually been performing best, and which have simply been lucky. This is extremely useful in betting, but is also useful for scouts trying to identify talented players. In order to demonstrate how Brentford have used Benham's Global Justice Table to master the transfer window, let's take the example of Scott Hogan.

When Brentford were promoted to the Championship in 2014, they were in dire need of attacking options. The two primary strikers who had got them promoted from League One had left the club, leaving them short of forward players. Benham asked his analysts at Smartodds to compile a shortlist of undervalued strikers whom Brentford might be able to pick up on the cheap.

The first step for Benham's data-driven recruitment team was to consult the Global Justice Table. Were there any lower league teams performing at a level much higher than their actual league position reflected? One team immediately sprang to the fore: Rochdale.

The innocuous League Two team had placed third in the fourth tier of English football, but Smartodds' Expected Goals data revealed that they were performing at an incredibly high level. The Global Justice Table had them ranked higher than many sides in the league above them. What was particularly noticeable was the number of high quality chances that the team were creating. They were accumulating impressively large Expected Goals totals every match. The data indicated that Rochdale's forwards were worth checking out.

Benham's analysts dug deeper. They studied the type of Expected Goals data which is outlined in Chapter 5 and Chapter 6 of this book. What was the driving factor behind Rochdale's performances? What kind of positions were they getting into? How were they amassing such large Expected Goals totals?

At the end of their analysis, they identified one key player who Rochdale's success was based upon: Scott Hogan. The striker was the driving force behind the League Two team's impressive performances. His Expected Goals data was unusually high for a striker of his level. After watching replays of his performances, Benham's recruitment team were satisfied that the data wasn't lying about his ability. Brentford snatched Hogan up for a measly £750k.

Fast-forward three years. Despite his time at Brentford being initially plagued with injury, Hogan had amassed twenty-one goals for the Bees in just thirty-three appearances. Matthew Benham realised that his stock was nearing its peak and sold him to Aston Villa for £12m. The transfer market maestros had once again used Expected Goals to beat the system.

It is clear that Brentford have benefitted greatly from Matthew Benham's ownership of Smartodds. But what specific unique advantages does the marriage of Brentford and Smartodds give Benham's football club?

First, Brentford have access to the most profound data. The Expected Goals method is the greatest analytical tool that can be used to drive player recruitment. Smartodds collect the highest quality data, which has allowed Brentford to successfully identify hidden gems. Meanwhile, other clubs tend to buy data from companies such as Opta. This data is accurate and useful, but does not provide the same level of insight as Smartodds' xG stats. In addition, the purchase of such data is often costly.

Second, Smartodds collects data on far more leagues than the typical stats company. Most clubs will only be able to access information on the top European leagues. Opta collect lots of different information points, but this restricts them in the number of divisions they can cover. Because they measure almost every conceivable data point (passes, tackles, blocks, headers, saves and so on) in the top European divisions, they don't have the resources to collect data on more obscure leagues. Smartodds, on the other hand, only collect Expected Goals data. They realise that this is the only metric they need to gauge team and player performance. Because such data is much more easily collected, they can collect it on far more teams and leagues than companies like Opta can. This grants them a greater pool of players from which they can spot talent. Indeed, Smartodds own the largest Expected Goals data resource worldwide (although, unfortunately, the only people with access to it are Brentford's analysts and the high-rolling bettors who use their services).

In fact, it is incredibly useful for Brentford that Smartodds possess data on a wide range of European leagues, as the club generally prefer to sign players from abroad. There are several reasons for this.

Firstly, the English football leagues are easily accessible to most managers and scouts. Even League Two, the lowest of the four tiers in professional English football, receives greater exposure than foreign leagues of the same playing standard. The average attendance in the English fourth tier surpasses that of the top divisions in many other European countries. Thus, there are very few "hidden gems" within English football. A great player languishing in the lower regions of the EFL will quickly be spotted and recruited by one of the top clubs. Just as bets on obscure European Leagues are of better value because the bookies pay less attention to such leagues, so too are the players of these leagues of better value because British scouts pay them less attention.

The second reason that Brentford have tended to sign foreign players is that they are a lot cheaper. The transfer fee for an English player will tend to be considerably more than the fee for a player of equal ability from a less accessible country. This seems counterintuitive. Why should one player be more expensive than the other when both are of equal ability?

The answer lies in the generally accepted notion that foreign players take a certain amount of time to acclimatise to the English Football League. It is regularly suggested that English football is a lot more physical and high tempo than other leagues around the world. Thus, when you pay for a player from another English club, you are paying for his ability *as well as* the fact that he has proven himself in the English game. Signing foreign players is seen as a risky manoeuvre because they may flop in the new playing environment.

Benham is sceptical of the belief that the English divisions are vastly different to the foreign leagues. Indeed, many of the foreign players that the Brentford owner has brought in have been huge successes in English football. Jota was bought from Spain for £1.5m, before being sold for £6m. Florian Jozefzoon was bought from Holland for £900k, before being sold for £2.8m. Maxim Colin was bought from France for £900k, before being sold for

£2m. Neal Maupay was bought from France for £1.6m, before becoming the Championship's second top scorer in 2018/19 and being sold for a whopping £20m.

There is no palpable evidence to suggest that players from abroad tend to struggle when they come over to England. Thus, transfer targets at other English clubs tend to be unnecessarily overvalued, prompting Brentford to look abroad to find the best deals.

Matthew Benham's transfer record at Brentford has been exceptional. The growth of the club has been founded on their ability to continually upgrade their squad. Sign players on the cheap, sell them for a profit, re-invest that money by buying more undervalued players, before selling them when they become overvalued. By repeating this cycle, Benham has been able to bring unprecedented on-field success to Brentford

Every team should follow Brentford's blueprint; the difficulty lies in actually identifying undervalued players. When everybody is trying to spot the diamond in the rough, the most sparkling of jewels will be quickly spotted by the clubs with the best recruitment networks. The top clubs have the most money to spend on infrastructure, but Brentford have managed to turn the tables through innovation. Benham's pioneering recruitment system based on the Expected Goals method has allowed Brentford to achieve success beyond their wildest dreams.

9

THE FUTURE OF xG

Where Does Football Analysis Go Next?

WHAT'S WRONG WITH EXPECTED GOALS?

There is no perfect way to analyse football. There are bad ways. There are good ways. There are the best ways. But there are no perfect ways. The Expected Goals method does have its flaws.

Chapter 4 and Chapter 5 of this book outline the ways in which we can use Expected Goals in team and player analysis. In order to collect their xG data, Opta draw upon a huge sample size of past shots in order to determine the success of a shot hitting the back of the net. In other words, if 10,000 shots were taken from a specific location and 1,000 of those shots resulted in a goal, then the probability of a future shot from that location resulting in a goal would be one in ten (10%). Thus, the shot would carry a value of 0.1(xG).

The position of the shot is the main determinant of its success, but Opta also incorporate a series of other factors into their model when assessing Shot Probability. Was the shooter on his stronger foot? Was the ball bouncing or was it motionless on the ground? Was the assist a cross, a pass or did the player assist himself? Was the effort a header? All these things affect the probability of the shot hitting the back of the net.

However, there are a series of problems with Opta's model.

First, we might question the accuracy with which an analyst can locate the position of a shot. Opta employ people to pinpoint the location of each shot on a digital pitch map. If the data logger misplaces the location of the shot by as little as a yard, the Shot Probability might inaccurately reflect the likelihood of the shot being scored. There are very few marks inside the penalty area of a football pitch, making it hard for analysts to accurately pinpoint the exact location from which a shot originated.

Second, Opta's model does not take into account the exact position of defenders or the goalkeeper. This drastically alters the likelihood of a shot hitting the back of the net. Clearly, a player shooting at an open net is far more likely to score than one shooting through a heavily crowded penalty area. Similarly, a player is more likely to score if the goalkeeper is out of position. These factors are not accounted for in Opta's Expected Goals model.

Third, threatening attacks regularly occur which do not produce shots. How often have you seen a dangerous ball across the face of goal narrowly miss the outstretched foot of a striker? How many times have you seen a forward just beaten to the ball by a goalkeeper flying out of his box? How many times have you seen an attacker round the goalkeeper, only to be forced too wide to take an attempt at goal? These are situations in which a team has clearly created an opportunity to score, but this will not be reflected in Opta's Expected

Goals data. When no shot actually takes place, no xG is afforded to the attacking team. This is problematic.

Fourth, own goals are not recognised. Similar to the third point, when a defender scores an own goal it is not picked up in the xG data. Own goals still represent a mistake by the opposition, a poor piece of defensive play or a good piece of attacking pressure. This should be reflected in the Expected Goals data. However, Opta's method is unable to incorporate this data. Because there is no actual shot taking place, the scoring opportunity is not represented in the xG.

A Better Expected Goals Method

These problems are very slight. Almost every company who collects Expected Goals data, of which there are few, uses the same method as Opta. This method still generates the most profound form of data which one can use to analyse football. The Expected Goals stats which you increasingly see displayed on football coverage and media platforms is still incredibly useful.

However, the slight problems with this form of Expected Goals annoyed Matthew Benham when he founded Smartodds in 2004. The professional gambler decided to develop his own brand of Expected Goals. The way he uses Expected Goals is the same as has been outlined in this book. He still generates Expected

Goals scorelines. He still converts these scorelines into Expected Points in the same way. Everything about Benham's xG methodology is the same, apart from how the data is actually *collected*. His brand of Expected Goals differs only in how each shot is measured.

Rather than drawing on a large computer database of past shots to determine the probability of a shot hitting the back of the net, Smartodds train their loggers to assess the probability for themselves. The employees who are tasked with logging the data are known as "Watchers". They are specially trained by the company to measure the *danger level* of each attack. *Dang*er is a key word which Smartodds highlight. Rather than knowing the probability of a shot resulting in a goal, they wish to understand the extent to which the defensive team have the situation under control. The level of danger is still translated into a probability that the attacking team will score, but it is not dependent on a shot taking place. Essentially, Smartodds measure the scoring probabilities of *attacks* rather than *shots*.

For example, suppose a striker rounds the goalkeeper but is pushed too wide to take a shot at goal. A Smartodds data logger would still note this as a dangerous chance. They would assign this opportunity a value – probably around 0.6(xG), as this is a very dangerous attack. Similarly, suppose a cross is whipped in across the face of goal, but is a yard in front of the onrushing attacker. No shot has taken place, but the logger might still assign this attack a value of around 0.3(xG). This reflects the fact that it was still a fairly dangerous situation.

Every attack is given a probability of succeeding. These xG values are still added up to reveal an Expected Goals scoreline. Smartodds data is still used in the exact same way as Opta's data. The only difference comes in the methodology of assessing the chances which take place.

Essentially, where Opta's analysts use computers to looks at a large sample of past shots to determine Shot Probabilities, Smartodds train actual human employees to measure the probability of each attack resulting in a goal. Opta measure *shots*, whist Smartodds measure *attacks*. There are a number of reasons why Smartodds' method is more intelligent.

First, a real life human who is watching football can see a lot more things than a computer can. Opta try to plug as many variables into their model as possible in order to form an accurate gauge of the value of a shot. Where was it taken from? Was it on the stronger foot? What was the assist type? However, a real person watching a shot can instantly get more of a sense of its scoring probability. They can see a number of things which the computer cannot. How well is the goalkeeper set? Was the shooter off-balance? How well were the defenders closing him down? Clearly, a Smartodds logger can provide a much more accurate reflection of scoring probabilities.

Second, Smartodds' analysts also have the ability to log attacks which don't end in shots. As highlighted above, Opta's data does not incorporate those dangerous situations in a football match which do not result in a shot being taken. Smartodds' data is much more profound as a result. Similarly, Smartodds' analysts can also log own goals. Opta's data will not recognise own goals as shots, but Smartodds' data will reveal these defensive mistakes.

The negative side of Smartodds' approach is that it is a slightly harder operation to carry out. The company have to provide regular training to their loggers in order to maintain the high quality of their data. It is not easy to train so many different "Watchers" to adjudge the value of each attack by the same set of rules. The company needs to calibrate each of their loggers' assessment of what constitutes a dangerous situation, or else their data will be inaccurate.

The other negative to Smartodds' approach is that their data is pretty useless for measuring individual player Expected Goals. They simply log xG data on teams, in order to form their domestic Justice Tables and Global Justice Table. They don't assign each Shot Probability to a player, but rather to the team as a whole. They believe that individual player Expected Goals data, such as is outlined in Chapter 6, does not offer useful enough insight to warrant collecting in any depth. Players do not take enough shots to produce meaningful enough xG sample sizes. It is much better to study the Expected Goals output of teams, then look within those high performing teams for star players.

For example, remember the example of how Scott Hogan was signed by Brentford. The analysts saw that Rochdale were creating many dangerous attacks going forward. They were amassing high Expected Goals totals each match. The analysts looked at why the team were performing so well and highlighted Scott Hogan as the underlying factor. Brentford signed him for £750k, and sold him for £12m two years later.

In conclusion, Smartodds' unique method for collecting Expected Goals data accounts for a lot more information than Opta's method. As such, it offers a more profound insight into the performance level of teams. However, it also offers a reconciliation between the traditionalist line of thought and the revolutionary line of thought which we have explored throughout this book. Yes, the method still relies on scientific data. But it also relies on human judgement. Because Smartodds ask the "Watchers" who log the data to assess the probability of each attack resulting in a goal, human inference is required to produce an accurate database. This offers a neat conciliation between art and science, between human and machine.

CONCLUSION

The Expected Goals method is a useful tool for predicting the outcome of future events. We can look at a team's past xG scorelines to work out the likelihood that they will win upcoming fixtures. However, even the Expected Goals method cannot predict how the future of football analytics will unravel. Where do we go from here?

The natural next step in the evolution of football analytics is prompting a greater engagement from fans and the media. As technology improves and better methods are devised of measuring performance, interest in a more scientific approach will increase. The Expected Goals method is currently an undervalued statistic. Once the media work out how to properly engage fans using xG, interest in the metric will grow.

With the increased exposure that the Expected Goals method will probably see over the next few years, xG will become more advanced. The current brand of Expected Goals analysis is by no means perfect. As more people become interested in its power, novel ways of using the metric will appear to surface. Perhaps the manner in which Smartodds collect Expected Goals will become the mainstream. Perhaps broadcasters will use this metric as their primary source of analysis during pre-match and post-match evaluation. Perhaps managers will begin to speak more openly about their teams' xG output.

There is still so much room for technology to influence football data. For instance, what's to stop the Football Association from authorising chips being put in match balls? This would allow analysts to detect the exact position of the ball, speed of the ball, curvature of the ball and several other variables at any point in a match. This would also greatly improve the quality of Expected Goals data. Inserting a chip inside a football would allow analysts to measure the exact position from which each shot is taken.

Additionally, inserting chips into the boots of each player on the pitch would allow analysts to track their exact position. An analyst with access to data on the exact location from which a shot was taken, data on the exact positioning of the defenders and goalkeeper when the shot was taken and data on how quickly the ball was moving when the striker hit it could more accurately work out the probability of the ball hitting the back of the net. More accurate Shot Probability readings would lead to more profound Expected Goals analysis.

Hawk-Eye is a computer system used in numerous sports to visually track the trajectory of the ball. Tennis and cricket have used Hawk-Eye in recent years to display a profile of the ball's most statistically likely path as a moving image. The system was developed by Paul Hawkins and was originally implemented in 2001 for television purposes in cricket. The system works via several high-performance cameras, normally positioned on the underside of the stadium roof, which track the ball from different angles. The video from the cameras is then triangulated and combined to create a three-dimensional representation of the ball's trajectory. Hawk-Eye is not infallible, but is accurate to within 3.6 millimetres. The system has recently been accepted by the governing bodies of association football in order to provide goal-line technology.

A further embracement and development of Hawk-Eye in football could greatly influence the development of the Expected Goals method. If Hawk-Eye is able to offer a representation of the trajectory of a cricket ball, surely the same could be done to a football? The system could be used to track every shot which takes place in a football match. This would supply data on the power with which each shot is hit, the curve that the striker manages to put on the ball and predict where blocked shots would have ended up. All these factors would enrich the Expected Goals data which we use to analyse football matches.

Artificial Intelligence is a hot trend in modern day computer science. AI is intelligence demonstrated by machines, in contrast to the natural intelligence displayed by humans. Colloquially, the term "Artificial Intelligence" is often used to describe computers that mimic the cognitive functions that humans associate with the human mind, such as learning and problem solving. Modern machine capabilities include successfully understanding human speech, computing at the highest level in strategic game systems such as chess, autonomously operating cars and intelligent routing in content delivery networks.

In football, Artificial Intelligence has the potential to bring revolutionary improvements. With the global industry starting to feel the shift towards automation, AI and football are building a strong relationship – from helping physios prevent concussion and ensuring a safer sport, to assisting referees in key decision-making. Who knows, in a few decades there may not be any need for human referees at all.

There is definite scope for the possibility of Artificial Intelligence being used to aid our quest for a smarter Expected Goals method. What if we could train computers to watch football matches and assess the quality of each attack which takes place? Companies would no longer have to employ loggers to collect Expected Goals data. Additionally, much more data could be collected on a greater variety of leagues.

Clearly, technological advances can revolutionise the nature of Expected Goals analysis. The resulting effect will be an exponentially positive cycle. As technology advances, more people would take interest in xG. As interest in Expected Goals grows, more people will come up with more intelligent ways of using it. As Expected Goals is used more intelligently, it will gain even more interest. This indefinite cycle can only be good for football analytics.

Positive change is certainly on the horizon. But what will never change is the fact that football is a sport in which lots of things happen at once. There are lots of independent factors which can impact a team's success. These factors are often very hard to measure, making it hard to get a clear picture of what is actually going right or wrong for a team. When over-performance or under-performance occurs, you have to work out if it is simply a result of luck or if something else is going on. Generally, we are too quick to put the blame on something substantial. We look for meaning in things where sometimes there is no meaning. We must accept that luck plays a huge role in the sport, and become better at accounting for that luck. This is what xG does: account for randomness and provide a clearer image of what is actually happening.

The Expected Goals method is a tool which can be used to measure the performance of teams. Fans can use it to select players for their Fantasy Football teams. Pundits can use it to provide more profound insight into their analysis. Scouts can use it to identify hidden gems. And the world of football can use it as a smarter language in which to talk about football.

BIBLIOGRAPHY

AFC Bournemouth 2014-15. (2015, May 4). Retrieved from Statto.com: http://www.statto.com/ football/teams/afc-bournemouth/2014-2015

Analysing the importance of Vincent Kompany to Manchester City. (2016, 1 12). Retrieved from Bleacher Report: http://bleacherreport.com/ articles/2606973-analysing-the-importance-of-vincent-kompany-to-manchester-city

Barnes, H. (2013, August 17). *Does It Make Statistical Sense to Sack a Football Manager?* Retrieved from BBC News: http://www.bbc.co.uk/news/ magazine-23724517

Coca-Cola Formula. (2015, Novemeber 7). Retrieved from Wikipedia: https://en.wikipedia.org/wiki/ Coca-Cola_formula

Flanagan, A. (n.d.). *Statistics Don't Always Tell the Whole Story.* Retrieved from The Mirror: http:// www.mirror.co.uk/sport/football/news/ arsene-wenger-statistics-dont-always-7040459

Hassan, N. (2013, October 26). *The Life of a Football Scout.* Retrieved from BBC Sport: http://www.bbc.co.uk/sport/0/football/24653124

Hytner, D. (n.d.). *Arsenal's Secret Signing.* Retrieved from The Guardian: https://www.theguardian.com/football/2014/oct/17/arsenal-place-trust-arsene-wenger-army-statdna-data-analysts

Innes, R. (2016, April 10). *11 Things That Were More Likely Than Leicester Winning the Premier League.* Retrieved from The Mirror: http://www.mirror.co.uk/sport/row-zed/11-things-were-officially-more-7320326

Innes, R. (2016, February 2016). *Gary Neville Record at Valencia.* Retrieved from The Mirror: http://www.mirror.co.uk/sport/row-zed/valencias-record-under-gary-neville-7327790

James, G. (2006). *Manchester City - The Complete Record.* Derby: Polar Publishing.

Leciester Fan Who Stakes £20 on Foxes Winning the Title Cashes Out. (2016, March 5). Retrieved from Mirror: http://www.mirror.co.uk/sport/other-sports/football/leicester-fan-who-staked-20-7497663

Manchester City F.C. Ownership and Finances. (n.d.). Retrieved from Wikipedia: https://en.wikipedia.org/wiki/Manchester_City_F.C._ownership_and_finances

Manchester City Transfers. (n.d.). Retrieved from
Transfer League: http://www.transferleague.
co.uk/manchester-city/english-football-teams/
manchester-city-transfers

Michu. (n.d.). Retrieved from Wikipedia: https://
en.wikipedia.org/wiki/Michu

Morris, B. (2014, July). *Billion-Dollar Billy Beane.*
Retrieved from FiveThirtyEight: http://fivethir-
tyeight.com/features/billion-dollar-billy-beane/

Morris, B. (2014, July 24). *Billion-Dollar Billy Beane.*
Retrieved from Fivethirtyeight: http://fivethir-
tyeight.com/features/billion-dollar-billy-beane/

MyFootballClub. (2016, March 9). Retrieved from
Wikipedia: https://en.wikipedia.org/wiki/
MyFootballClub

Page, D. (n.d.). *Expected Goals Just Don't Add Up.*
Retrieved from https://medium.com/@danny-
page/expected-goals-just-don-t-add-up-they-
also-multiply-1dfd9b52c7d0#.ecnn3zbyu

Penalty Practice For England. (2012, June 21). Retrieved
from Yahoo! Sport: https://uk.sports.yahoo.
com/news/penalty-practice-england-065427414.
html

Red Hair. (n.d.). Retrieved from Wikipedia: https://
en.wikipedia.org/wiki/Red_hair

Remembering Michu. (n.d.). Retrieved from
SB Nation: http://www.sbnation.
com/soccer/2015/11/9/9696572/

michu-released-swansea-city-2012-13-season-22-goals

Simendinger, T. (2011, October 27). *Why First Impressions Are Hard to Change.* Retrieved from Ocean Palmer: http://oceanpalmer.com/2011/10/why-first-impressions-are-hard-to-change/

Sorene, P. (2013). *The History of Football Goalposts.* Retrieved 2015, from Who Ate All The Pies: http://www.whoateallthepies.tv/retro/158123/the-history-of-football-goal-posts.html

Standard Deviation. (n.d.). Retrieved from Wikipedia: https://simple.wikipedia.org/wiki/Standard_deviation

Stuart, K. (2014, 8 12). *Why clubs are using Football Manager as a real life scouting tool.* Retrieved from The Guardian: http://www.the-guardian.com/technology/2014/aug/12/why-clubs-football-manager-scouting-tool

Taylor, D. (2014, July 3). *Massimo Cellino Axes Paddy Kenny from Leeds Over Date of Birth.* Retrieved from The Guardian: http://www.theguardian.com/football/2014/jul/03/massimo-cellino-leeds-united-paddy-kenny

Taylor, M. (2014, February 12). *The Power of Goals.* Retrieved from http://thepowerofgoals.blogspot.co.uk/2014/02/twelve-shots-good-two-shots-better.html

The Millenial Sim is Here. (2015, August). Retrieved from
Reddit: https://www.reddit.com/r/footballma-
nagergames/comments/3fioa1/the_millenial_
sim_is_here_1000_years_of_simming/

The Statistical Fairy Enchants Football. (n.d.).
Retrieved from Reddit: https://m.red-
dit.com/r/soccer/comments/1jj3es/
the_statistical_fairy_enchants_football/

Weather Forecasting Through the Ages. (n.d.). Retrieved
from Earth Observatory: http://earthobserva-
tory.nasa.gov/Features/WxForecasting/wx2.php

What is ExpG? (n.d.). Retrieved from 11tegen11:
http://11tegen11.net/2014/02/10/what-is-expg/

Williams, J. (2009, April 22). *Penalty Kicks By
The Numbers.* Retrieved from Science of
Soccer: http://www.scienceofsocceronline.
com/2009/04/penalty-kicks-by-numbers.html

Williams-Grut, O. (2016, February 10). *Inside
Starlizard.* Retrieved from Business
Insider: http://uk.businessinsider.com/
inside-story-star-lizard-tony-bloom-2016-2

Influential Works

Anderson, Chris and David Sally, *The Numbers Game: Why Everything You Know About Football is Wrong* (Viking, London, 2013)

Buchdahl, Joseph, *Squares & Sharps, Suckers & Sharks* (High Stakes Publishing, Herts, 2016)

Ferguson, Alex, *My Autobiography* (Bantam Books, London, 2007)

Haigh, John, *Taking Chances* (Oxford University Press, New York, 2009)

Hornby, Nick, *Fever Pitch* (Indigo, London, 1996)

Kuper, Simon and Stefan Szymanski, *Soccernomics* (HarperSport, London, 2014)

Lewis, Michael, *Moneyball* (W.W. Norton & Company Ltd., New York, 2004)

Peace, David, *The Damned United* (Faber and Faber, London, 2006)

Silver, Nate, *The Signal and the Noise: The Art and Science of Prediction* (Allen Lane, London, 2012)

Taylor, Peter, *With Clough by Taylor* (Sidgwick & Jackson, London, 1980)

Tomkins, Paul, Graeme Riley and Gary Fulcher, *Pay as You Play: The True Price of Success in the Premier League Era* (GPRF Publishing, Wigston, 2010)

Made in the USA
Columbia, SC
24 May 2021

38475615R00133